A Girl and Her Money

A Girl and Her Money

Sharon Durling

W Publishing Group™

www.wpublishinggroup.com

A Division of Thomas Nelson, Inc.
www.ThomasNelson.com

Published by W Publishing Group, a division of Thomas Nelson, Inc., P.O. Box 141000, Nashville, Tennessee 37214.

Unless otherwise indicated, Scripture quotations are from The Holy Bible, New International Version (NIV). Copyright © 1973, 1978, 1984, International Bible Society. Used by permission of Zondervan Bible Publishers.

ISBN 0-8499-4376-0

Printed in the United States of America
03 04 05 PHX 9 8 7 6 5 4 3 2

Contents

ACKNOWLEDGMENTS

THIS BOOK HAS BEEN PATIENTLY WAITING TO BREAK out for a while. I am grateful to Todd Sinelli and Stacey Padrick Thompson for urging me to write it and set it free. Warmest thanks to senior editor Ami McConnell for her professionalism, guidance, and spirit. And more than a nod to editor Holly Halverson for her (desperately needed) organizational skills.

Thanks to Joan and Brandt Madsen, Jeanie and David Hoover, Marla Mothershed, Kevin Tobin, Beth Hart, and Marnie and Dan Hanesworth, for their loving hospitality in this, the most amazing of years for me.

Thanks to my assortment of beautiful friends whose support, words, and love sustain my spirit, mind, and heart: Melissa Copley, Nora Moreno Cargie, Cathleen Tobin, Mary Ann Wilkens, Bill Pavelec, Dana Sweeney, Eva Hyndman, Dody Finch, Susan Cheng, Greg King, and Wanda Taylor. Thanks to Dave Jones for tech and lunch support.

I am grateful to my wonderful and functional Family Durling for their prayers—especially Marilyn, Carol, Sally, Donald, Zita, Calvin, JoAnn, and Philip. Most especially am I grateful to my mother and dad, for their love and example that continue to amaze me as well as any bystanders along the way.

Thanks to Rev. James T. Meeks, from whom I am still learning the power of praying big prayers.

A Brief and Painless Analogy

HOW ARE YOUR TEETH? MINE ARE GREAT. TWICE a year, Mom took me to Doc Taylor's office overlooking Main Street where he would tell me I had maybe one cavity, the rest looked great, and I should keep flossing. Eighty-some dental visits later, they're beautiful, and because they're my only set, I treat all thirty of them very well (two belligerent molars started a fight and had to go).

I do the same for my car. It goes to Milito's for a regular oil change because I figure if I'm good to my car, it'll be good to me. I brush the winter salt off my shoes and buff them to make that leather look great one more season. My silks and wools travel regularly to the dry cleaner to ensure they retain their shape and longevity. The heating/cooling guy sees my furnace and air conditioner annually, checking Freon levels and CO output, ensuring the health and safety of my house and me.

I love my body (it's my only one) and cherish my relatively good health. I see my internist, gynecologist, mammogram technician, and dermatologist for checkups. I hope to keep myself in exceptional condition through old age. My fuel intake reflects this: I avoid dairy products, processed flours and sugars, caffeine, and alcohol, and opt instead for vegetables, fruits, and soy things. I take herbs to boost my immune system. I exercise and do yoga to keep back pain, mental sluggishness, and other stuff I don't want at bay.

I tend to my spiritual health as well. I meditate, read the Bible, and get appropriately, uncomfortably challenged by my minister, all of which help to keep me spiritually strong.

I get lots of love from my social circle; I return the love and do volunteer work.

My life—most of the time—is fairly well-rounded. OK, this is embarrassing to admit, so go easy on me, but I'll tell you the truth: I have been less inclined to take as meticulous care of my capital assets as I have my merino wool sweater with the marinara sauce spilled down the front. I'll rush that sweater right over to Don's Cleaners. I'll run my car over to Milito's at the first funny sound in the engine. I dash out for decongestants at the first sense of heaviness in my sinuses. I call my friends at the first whiff of a blue mood. I resew loose buttons, fertilize my flowers, and keep my bicycle oiled. The truth is, I don't always care for my financial assets as well as I do my body, house, clothes, and car.

So years went by before I bothered to notice I was paying 28 cents per minute for long-distance calls. Meanwhile, the rest of you had figured out the call-pack plans of your local and long-distance carriers and were averaging 4.2 cents per minute from

Jacksonville to Juneau. Sometimes all you have to do is actually read those statements.

Sign of the Times

As if bound for Oprah-land, we women of the third millennium are fixated on holistic balance in our lives—mental, emotional, spiritual, and physical health. Yet notoriously, our financial health is left wanting. As chicklets who just want to have fun, we don't really want to think about the fact that we outlive the men in our lives and have smaller pension plans because we tend to get paid less and work fewer years. The fact is, dear sweet girl on the go, you do not want to wake up someday to discover your physical assets have outlived your financial assets—*yikes!* So we must give both equal care. In fact, excellent physical health will positively impact your financial health—healthcare expense can be a huge drain on your finances. Moreover, financial dis-ease has been known to instigate physical illness.

So if I keep taking such good care of my body, and if I inherited longevity genes from Grandma Durling—who was fit as a fiddle till she died of an infected toe in her 107th year—and if I could just quit my jaywalking habit, it's altogether likely I'll be sprinting into my nineties. So it's all the more important that I do the same for my financial assets as I do for my teeth, merino sweater, and car—that I know where my finances are, with whom they are cavorting, whether they need a new spark plug, some cleaning solution, braces, or a vaccination.

The bottom line is this: Why would you take excellent care of your teeth—assuming you do, oh sweet-breathed one—and not ensure that the result of your lifetime work is also kept in sparkly white, cavity-free condition, fully protected from rot, thievery, and an early demise?

It's All about You

You see, what you do today profoundly affects your future. You must make financial decisions as if your life depended on it. In fact—it *does*. The tiniest of decisions add up to a critical mass that can make or break your financial future. What you think about, and therefore what actions you take now, profoundly impacts your future.

Money isn't easy. It is as complicated as any relationship. It requires the attention, nurture, and communication demanded of a marriage. But the investment of your time and attention always pays: Attending to your relationship with money will bring greater satisfaction to your life. Maybe you and your money will even attend a few counseling sessions together. By calling for a peaceful truce with your finances, you will dissolve distaste for paying bills, contributing to your retirement fund, and giving to charity. In fact, you'll look forward to opportunities to give and save.

When you see money as your friend or sibling, you'll want to work to make that relationship succeed. It's all about the relationship—your feelings about money, your behavior with it, and your respect for it. When you give up trying to control money and can relax around it, you will view it differently. From your new perspective, you'll see your little bits of money as something in your favor, there to please and suit *you*.

Why *not* fall in love with your money? Because it doesn't work that way. Sometime around the tenth century B.C., a wise King

Solomon spoke the truth: "Whoever loves money never has money enough; whoever loves wealth is never satisfied."[1] I don't want a lifetime of singing "I Can't Get No Satisfaction." Let's discover how to have money, perhaps even become wealthy, but attain a sense of satisfaction and joy all the while.

Your Destiny: Financial Freedom

A life of financial freedom surely does not include many of the emotions that bubble to the surface when you scurry past the personal finance section of a bookstore, when your credit card bill arrives, or when you flip open a mail-order catalog to the digital video camera you can't have. Yet there is no reason why you cannot have a happy, healthy, and fulfilling relationship with money. There is no reason why you cannot experience freedom from financial worries.

Life is not meant for us to be distraught over unpaid bills, wear duct-taped shoes, and put our children to bed hungry. We should relish the fruits of our labor. We should enjoy and be satisfied with our possessions and not perpetually crave more. We were not put on this planet to struggle in pain and anxiety over financial problems.

It's OK if you've got money tension. Tension, you see—the yin and yang of life—is good. Without it, there's little joy. The tension of piano or violin strings offers sweet harmony. Loosely relaxed strings offer only a dull thud. So you're normal. It's all a part of our managing, measuring, balancing, and being.

I *so* hope you will learn to live with the tension in a healthy way that brings true harmonic resonance to your life. No matter how well or poorly you currently maintain your finances—or whether you maintain them at all—you can experience the wonders of financial freedom.

To help you do this, let's walk through some basic steps— identifying your money personality, doing a financial checkup, identifying good and bad debt, taming the shopping shrew, defining true wealth, understanding the power of good planning, and making peace with money. Along the way, I'll share personal stories showing how others and I have learned valuable lessons through our difficult times with money. I will help you get off to a roaring start on the road to financial freedom.

Know that I speak as a fellow student. I believe we teach what we need to learn. I still suffer some angst about money. There is no way I have it entirely wrapped up and figured out, but I'm well along the path toward peace with money. I admit I would be severely challenged were I faced with a devastating financial loss and bankruptcy. It would be a huge test of my faith and what I teach. But I'll not let the fact that I'm imperfect and susceptible to failure prohibit me from sharing the things I've learned and observed with you.

C. S. Lewis said it is at least worth lending an ear to "a fellow-patient in the same hospital who, having been admitted a little earlier, could give some advice."[2] Dear sweet reader, I'm only a patient in the next room who would love to give you the heads-up on a couple of things I've picked up in my short stay here.

So get ready to give your financial health a good look. Be prepared to do a little maintenance and call in the professionals when necessary. Take a read on your cash "oil gauge," polish your portfolio, and brush and floss your budget to ensure the long-term health of your finances. Take baseline measures of your financial situation so you will be able to track your progress year after year, recognize trends in symptoms and disease, and learn why, when, and how to achieve your goals. Education—accurate information—is a first step on the way to excellent financial health, and you can get it.

Start with a checkup, and schedule them regularly. Then engage in preventative treatment: Scrub away the tartar, check for gum disease, get fluoride treatment, and purge the cavities *before* they rot those teeth. Then sit back and enjoy your pearly whites—for a lifetime of abundance and peace of mind.

CHAPTER ONE

The Funny Thing about Money

money and you

Take a moment to consider:

- What emotions does money stir within you? Is the thought of money inclined to stir excitement or depression?

- What language and expressions do you use concerning money and possessions? Do you often say, "I can't afford it"? When you make a purchase, do you tend to moralize, saying, "I was really bad" or "I was good this time"? Do you say, "I can't manage money; I just can't get ahead"?

- Have you allowed money to damage or destroy a relationship?

- Are you too busy to think about money? What does it take for your finances to get your attention?

- If you had more money, what additional options would you have for freedom, time, choices, or career? What increased insecurity might it bring?

WHAT HAS THE FORCE OF A TSUNAMIC WAVE, THE seduction of a gorgeous guy, and the mystery of—well, life itself? What drives sane men mad and to death at their own hands? What has the power to stop herds of stampeding men and women dead in their tracks, is more thrilling than the World Series, and is a force for which many will forgo their marriage vows, children, even their own identity?

Money.

So what *is* it with money? It triggers a barrage of emotions. It influences many of the decisions we make, from what we eat to whom we marry, whether we divorce, where we live, and the careers we pursue. It stirs feelings of guilt, fear, dissatisfaction, anxiety, panic, greed, misery, ecstasy, confidence, and hope. It affects our sense of success, security, self-esteem, independence, acceptance, and even love. Personal finance tomes appear frequently on bestseller lists. Books about money outsell books on sex. Magazines and newsletters devoted to the acquisition and management of money proliferate. And how many different channels are there of money TV?

Money brings out the amazing in us. It can cause a pacifist to fight to the death, impel a mother to cut off her son, and influence a girl to fall in love with a cranky man her grandfather's age.

It is a store of information about a person—her background, family relationships, schooling, principles, and more. In our monetarily repressed culture, people often will not disclose their incomes to their families, friends, or fiancés. It is a culture in which people will be sexually intimate far more readily than they will be fiscally revealing.

Money is good; money is bad. Money is detestable; money is incorrigible. Money is freedom, money is the answer, and money is sexual. Whatever the truth about money, one thing I know: In one form or another, it's here to stay. So we'd better learn to live with it. The sooner we learn to get along with money—both ours and the Joneses'—the sooner we can make peace with this thing called cash.

The Problem with Money

Money is a big fat liar. So don't even start to believe her. True, money's a nonorganic object, but we've nearly elevated her to family matriarch. When she's flaunting herself, she gives us a high much like that swell we felt with our first grade-school infatuation. Likewise, she deflates our spirits when she makes scarce. Delilah-like, she seduces by claiming that if you love and acquire her, she'll bring you more happiness and satisfaction than you could possibly imagine. Although her titillating whispers never quite deliver as promised, we continue to lean deeply into her, hopeful for more assurances from her collagen-injected lips. Bystanders of post-modern culture have a few things to say about her.

Clinical Psychologist

Richard Ryan, Ph.D., professor at the University of Rochester: "There's a very short half-life to the pleasure that comes from spending."[3] By the time the new earrings are out of the tissue and into the jewelry box, they've already lost a little of their thrill.

Ever notice that when you're going to a party, you feel better wearing a new silk shirt than an old one; even when the old one fit just a bit better and

> Money hasn't any value of its own; it represents the stored up energy of men and women and is really just someone's promise to pay a certain amount of that energy.
> ✳ *Laura Ingalls Wilder* ✳

looked better with those pants? Wearing a new dress to a wedding just feels grander than a dress you've worn before. Three wearings, and it's demoted to the back of the closet.

Shopaholic

Middle-aged woman to sales clerk at a boutique in Chicago's Lincoln Park neighborhood: "Wow, I feel so much better. I was feeling so blah today I just had to get out and buy *something* for a pick-me-up."

To that I'd say, "Might as well shoot up some drugs while you're at it." A fix is a fix.

Media Mogul

Ted Turner said, "I bet you're all wondering what it feels like to be a billionaire. It's disappointing really. . . . I've learned that great wealth isn't nearly as good as average sex."[4]

Hmmm. If Ted's right, and if we can assume the average person could achieve average sex, we can therefore conclude the average person feels as awesome now as if he had a billion dollars. Wow—

how ordinary is that? So money *won't* buy me love, coolness, freedom, independence, and wake me up with a big smile on my face?

Fiancée of an English Heir

"I thought about all that would someday be mine—heirloom silver, imported rugs, family jewels, a chauffeur. *Is this it?* I wondered. *Are possessions what life is all about?* I began to question my values."[5]

This woman received a gift most people don't get until old age, if then. She recognized in her youth that money and the possessions it offers would not satisfy, and as a result, she was propelled into clarifying her values apart from the fineries in her life. She broke off the engagement.

Comic Strip Creator

Workplace philosopher and *Dilbert* cartoonist Scott Adams said, "If all the people who were buying things that have no utility whatsoever realized they have no utility, the economy would collapse."[6]

So why do we buy? Why do we so desperately want more things that have no real use? Surely it's for our own self-interest; none of us is so benevolent as to spend solely in the interest of furthering our nation's economy. It occurred briefly post–September 11, but patriotism is not ordinarily our motivation to shop. The purveyors of such "useless" objects promote the idea that acquiring them will give us a big "happy" quotient.

The problem with money is that it promises things it cannot deliver.

Money as Obstacle, Narcotic, Distraction

The other thing about money is that it gets in the way of our ability to see reality. Like a barrier, it blocks our ability to discover and confront our problems. We don't want to see the unpleasantness of our reality. Getting or having a great deal of money often simply delays our discovering the source of unhappiness, and therefore actually impedes the journey toward a solution to our problems.

We use it as a panacea for depression and marital and family conflict. We use money and all the stuff it affords us as a tranquilizer or anesthetic to block the real pain underneath. We try to numb our sadness and disappointment with the possessions money offers, much like narcotics mask physical pain. A life anesthetized is one that settles for mediocrity, at best.

We also allow money to distract us, making us unaware of our spiritual needs and numbing our spiritual appetites. When we transfer all of our desire, hope, and security from the spiritual to the material realm, our spiritual self starves into anorexia. We lose touch with that side of ourselves.

We do funny things with money. We feast, then fast; we gorge and discard; we splurge, then we cut back. Both the wealthy and poor, in varying degrees of desperation, are in search of the salve to end the cycle. Investment guides propel some readers into deeper despair when they realize they'll never retire before seventy-five—much like an alcoholic who gets so spooked at an AA meeting that she strides right out for a stiff drink. Unchecked compulsions to earn, spend, or hoard money have resulted in emotional, relational, and spiritual paupers.

Getting more money, contrary to popular thought, will not solve our problems. In fact, if all your problems can be solved with money, you need to reassess your definition of *problem*. Some lottery winners, within a few years of hitting the jackpot, become broke, overweight, depressed, divorced, and worse. The winnings serve as an amplifier of a person's true self.

"How far," wondered author Jacob Needleman, "has money become an instrument of emotional expression in our lonely society—a language of the emotions, the only such language left for many of us?"[7] This is not a phenomenon exclusive to our current capitalistic economy. The prophet Isaiah asked rhetorically, "Why spend money on what is not bread, and your labor on what does not satisfy?"[8]

Why indeed? If money buys security, why did lottery winner Charles Tabet say, "Now that I have this much money, I think I need more money to be secure"?[9] And why did the magazine cover title on celebrities filing for bankruptcy proclaim, "Going Broke on $33 Million a Year"?[10]

If money buys freedom, why do some of the *über* rich live out their years as recluses and barricade themselves behind gates, alarm systems, and bodyguards?

If money buys friends, why, when Doris Duke died, did she have "no relatives or friends she particularly cared to enrich"[11] with her $1.2 billion estate?

If it is prestige, why did Charles F. Feeney give away $3.5 billion *anonymously*, keeping less than $5 million of his vast fortune for himself?[12]

Your choice is—and, girlfriend, the good news is, *you do get to choose*—to be content or not.

Money's OK—Really, It Is!

So is there anything good about money? Can we relax and just spend a little already? Absolutely. It's not about the money anyway. It's what's in your head—what you think about and believe—that matters.

Money's not bad. So get yourself some! Having, saving, borrowing, and spending money has occured all through history. In biblical times, God gave people great monetary wealth and, even better, the ability to totally enjoy it![13] Lose the false guilt about having and enjoying.

There are times, however, when money and possessions are taken away—even from those who are generous and kind (see the story of Elijah in 1 Kings, chapter 17, and Job, chapter 1). Therefore, contrary to what some television preachers may tell you, you can safely conclude your net worth is not a direct correlation of God's approval or disapproval. God often blesses in ways far greater than monetary riches and punishes in ways far broader than removing wealth. Sadly, sometimes the more arrogant and wicked people are, the wealthier they get.[14]

The writer of a best-selling book posed the question, "Does God want Christians to have money?" Do you think God wants people to engage in sex and enjoy food and drink? Let's hope so! I believe God created all of these, as well as the network that has evolved into our complex monetary system today. Improper management of money, improper management of food, and improper engagement in sex are destructive and wrong. Gorging, purging, and self-starvation are disrespectful and harmful to our bodies. No question—even disrespectful sex within marriage is wrong. Need I mention credit card bloat?

It's about balance. It's about moderation. Gratuitous and abusive sex is wrong. Money and food are often grossly misused. Food, money, and sex exist for people to thoroughly enjoy. We can honor ourselves and others in the way we appropriately use and participate in all three.

God not only created my desires, but he continues to have an active interest in me, and my money: my rent, bulging credit card bills, and IRA rollover account. That's a relief, given the volatility I've seen in my stock portfolio. (So you don't have a portfolio? Those bills stuffed in the quart jar on the top shelf are equally important.)

I believe God is fully interested in my monetary life, yet he leaves the choice to me: to master money or be its slave.

There's Freedom in Surrender

Let's go back to those questions at the beginning of the chapter. Where are you in the financial quagmire? Are money issues a source of stress or merely another item on your to-do list? Perhaps you're reading this book because you want some insight on better handling this weighty beast. The first truth toward that end is this: Freedom over money is acquired by relinquishing our attachment to it—thus the term *financial freedom*.

That indicates freedom *from* money, not freedom *because of* money. Oh, but a preposition has never made such a big divide in meaning. If a lot of money were required to be free, then most of us could never aspire to financial freedom. When we give less power to the money we have (and the money we don't have, but wish we did), we gain freedom to think differently. As mere mortals, we give a lot of power to things that are not in our control—to events over which we can do nothing. What a waste of our precious and limited energy. To win in life, to have all the happiness we want, we must learn the art of letting go.

We know this: When a man breaks our heart, our feelings don't simply disappear. What we must do, however, is to let go of the relationship in our thought process. In my mind, I forgive the guy, bless him, and move my thoughts to something more pleasant. Over time, the pain fades. When that driver cuts us off with a wave of her finger, it's a waste to give her one bit of our valuable emotional energy. When the Fed raises interest rates two days before our mortgage interest rate was to be set, we do best not to think about last week's lower rates.

Thinking differently causes changes in our feelings. Changes in our feelings cause us to change our actions. Changes in our actions bring us to different results. Do you want different results from your financial management—your shopping, saving, spending, investing, and check floating? Writer Anne Lamott said, "Truth is usually a paradox—that freedom is found in surrender, for instance, or that he who loses life shall gain it."[15]

> A man's riches may ransom his life, but a poor man hears no threat.
>
> ✳ *Proverbs 13:8* ✳

Only when you are willing to completely let go of something you think you possess can you take security in it. Only when you are willing to give up control of your child, husband, or boyfriend can you rest in the certainty that his devotion is true. So you win by giving up.

Successful Wall Street traders get this. They are far more profitable when they have the ability to accept trading losses and not become emotionally trapped in a declining investment. They warn, "Don't get married to your position"—that is, the stock or bond you bought that's performing badly, but you're just *sure* will see the light of day soon, simply because you like it so much. Some traders will tell you they are successful not because they have the ability to consistently pick the best stocks, but because they have the ability to let go of a bad position. That is critical to a trader's success. When she learns to confidently and quickly cut her losses, she'll consistently outperform other traders who may be smarter but are emotionally less able to sell a poor performer.

The ability to let go is the hallmark of a great trader, but it's also a hallmark of great strength and character. Jesus intimated that until you diminish your attachment to your portfolio value, you cannot experience freedom (see Luke 16:13). Those loyalties must be shorn to understand true financial liberty.

In 1994, I visited a refugee camp in Thailand near the Mekong River. Thousands of people lived in long buildings with little privacy and no security. Some refugees arrived destitute. Others attempted to bring their wealth (usually in gold) as they escaped Laos by swimming across the river. Which group do you think was more likely to drown? Who do you think slept most easily at night? Of course, those who brought gold lived in constant fear it would be stolen.

This, then, the paradox of letting go, is the first step to financial freedom, wherever you find yourself on the freaked-out-by-money chart. Leo Tolstoy was right when he wrote, "True life is lived when tiny changes occur." That's all you have to do—just one small thing differently than you've done in the past. Satisfaction, hope, and peace of mind are within your reach. It is more possible than you may think.

Let's Get Started

Here are some "tiny changes" you can make to start giving money less power in your life—to let go of finances so you can embrace freedom:

- As if you need to be told: Leave your credit cards at home for one week, or even a month.

- Replace one thing this week, such as lunch from home for lunch in a restaurant, or a book from the library for a new paperback you'd intended to buy.
- Volunteer to serve one meal at a homeless shelter or mission near you.
- Give a gift such as an evening of babysitting to a single parent this week.
- This week, give a large gift of money anonymously to someone whom you know to be in need. (You could send a cashier's check, or leave an envelope of cash in a front-door mail slot.)
- Pick up a *Wall Street Journal*, if you don't ordinarily, and read several articles in the "Money and Investing" section.
- Read just one chapter from a book on investing this week from the library.
- Next time you get the urge to splurge, browse in a consignment shop before heading to the mall or neighborhood boutiques.
- Spend guiltlessly! Take ten or even a hundred bucks, and buy something you would not ordinarily get for yourself.
- As you might pray a blessing before a meal, pray as you deposit money in the bank (or receive your employee automatic deposit statement) that the money would bless your life.
- Pray that you would have the ability to use your money wisely and productively for enjoyment and to good purpose.

"Action breeds action" is the mantra of my career-counselor friend. An object in motion tends to stay in motion, postulated Sir Isaac Newton. (You figured this out well before tenth-grade physics, the first time your pudgy little hand slammed down on a plastic ball and it rolled out of reach, leaving you baffled and wailing for your mama.) "The smaller the movement, the more profound the effect," said Peter Hays on the Feldenkrais method, which trains the body to heal itself by relearning body movement and awareness. Peter says, "Basically, after an injury or getting stuck in a myopic rut, the body forgets that it has other options, that it is able to move differently, move better, and feel better." Within twenty-four hours of reading this chapter, take some action in your financial life, breeding more positive action.

> To change one's life:
> Start immediately, do it
> flamboyantly. No exceptions.
> ∗ William James ∗

Reawaken your movements.

You see, if you begin to make small changes in your thinking and attitude, like the tiniest muscle movement correcting your posture and alleviating pain, so will these seemingly miniscule changes in your thoughts and feelings about money act to alleviate severe fiscal disarray and pain. Financial freedom is your destiny. Come and get it!

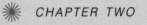

CHAPTER TWO

Your Money Personality— and You Do Have One

money and you

Take a moment to consider:

- Are you a compulsive hoarder or spender? Do you get more enjoyment from spending or saving?
- Are you risk averse, holding your money too tightly in a low-interest-bearing bank account?
- Are you an avoider, hoping that if you look away, somehow your financial situation will self-correct?
- Do you spend hours clipping coupons, elated at each additional dime you save?
- Do you feel a familiar surge of excitement when stepping into a beautiful department store, contented when you leave with your arms full of crisp new tissue-lined shopping bags?
- When it comes to your finances, do you experience feelings of ignorance, fear, guilt, frustration, incompetence, unworthiness, anxiety, insecurity, worry, thrill, excitement, pride, hope, or discontent?

YOUR MONEY PERSONALITY IS SIMPLY THE FEELINGS, reactions, and behaviors you exhibit when it comes to all things financial. What is yours like?

Let's face it. People are weird about money, and there are as many nuances to how people act with money as there are grains of sand on the beach. Liza Hughes's story was printed in the *New York Times*:

I got on a downtown train loaded with two bags of groceries. The only open seat was filled with a large shopping bag belonging to a very well-dressed young woman. "Excuse me, may I sit there?" I asked. "Do you have to?" she almost hissed. Feeling angry and a little intimidated, I was relieved to hear a young man next to her say, "Excuse me, but do you think your bag deserves a seat over a person?"

"But it's a $3,000 dress," she said.

The young man and I replied at the same time, "Then you should have taken a taxi."

She moved her bag.[16]

My money personality has its own idiosyncrasies. Take a look at how my perspective has developed.

My Money Personality

At three weeks of age, I had my own savings account with ten dollars my grandparents gave me just for showing up. When I was six, I earned two cents each time I washed or dried dishes. At ten, I earned two dollars for memorizing the twenty-eighth chapter of Matthew. (This will come in handy if I'm ever in a POW camp without a Bible.)

> I started out with nothing. Luckily, I still have most of it left.
>
> * Jill Petzke *

At ten, I parceled out my meager finances in percentages for saving, spending, and giving. I divided a little plastic jewelry case into sections with cardboard strips and tape, carefully marking each of the three categories. I still keep records and have added loads of categories (taxes, mortgage payments, etc.) but the plastic box has been replaced with Microsoft Excel.

During college years, however, my money personality changed. Looming tuition bills without resources to meet them took a toll on me. I worked overtime and my grades suffered. I never made a long-distance phone call (my mother sent letters), had no late-night pizza, took no spring-break trips with my roommates, and sewed my own clothes. I was happy to get a job on the night shift assembling automobile air-conditioning parts and inspecting the little tubes that windshield-wiper fluid shoots out of.

Thus was my craving for financial security whetted. I never wanted to be caught so close to the bottom again. I began to take out student loans for just a wee bit more than I actually needed so

I would always have a spare C-note or two. I came close but never missed making my bill payments. Over time, the cushion I've needed to feel secure has grown as my income has upwardly mobilized.

I began saving from my first day on the job. I was twenty-three and paying $295 in monthly rent and $75.53 in student loan payments. My annual salary was $11,800. I added the $20 or $40 I eked out per month to the savings I had earned from being born.

In my adulthood, I live by the mantra "No income, no outgo."

Everything appears great, but here's the truth: I still crave the security my financial assets provide. I'm inconsistent in monitoring my retirement savings and investments, in spite of my storied Wall Street career and coursework in portfolio management at a premier business school. My knuckles turn white as I cling to my stock portfolio. I clutch the coins in my pocket until my hand muscles cramp. When I call to negotiate a job offer, to ask for a higher salary or a bigger sign-on bonus, I tremble as if calling for an oncology report.

Money is, for me, a high-stakes game. I've cried over my lack of money as a college student when tuition bills loomed like a three-headed monster. I've been red-hot angry with siblings over what I believed to be their lack of consideration toward me on money matters. I've been elated when cash I was not expecting has wended itself my way. Much of my life I have been, frankly, stuck on money.

Your Early Money Experiences

Your own money personality developed during your financially formative years—the first decade of your life. It was formed by your childhood experiences. To better understand your own money personality, hark yourself back to when you were ten years old.

Your family and cultural money history affected your beliefs about money. What you learned then has profoundly impacted your relationships with friends, your spouse, children, charitable organizations, and the poor in your community, as well as helped to formulate your political beliefs and view of sister nations around the globe. Use the following quiz to ascertain where your own beliefs about money came from.

My Money History

Indicate True or False

( ) T ( ) F   1. My parents often argued with one another about money issues.

( ) T ( ) F   2. I was aware that my parents were worried about bills.

( ) T ( ) F   3. Discussing money was taboo in my family.

( ) T ( ) F   4. My parents lied to one another about money, e.g., my mother might deny that a new dress she was wearing was, in fact, new.

( ) T ( ) F   5. I had no money of my own to spend, save, or tithe.

( ) T ( ) F   6. I was not aware whether my parents used credit cards, had a mortgage or car payments, etc.

( ) T ( ) F   7. I did not receive an allowance nor earn money for chores or odd jobs at home or elsewhere.

( ) T ( ) F   8. My parents suffered financially and lost investments or filed for bankruptcy.

( ) T ( ) F   9. I felt my family's financial status was different than it really was, i.e., we had wealth, but I thought we were poor; or we were poor, but I didn't realize it.

( ) T ( ) F   10. Money was used as a means of control, with a system of rewards and punishments in place, thus connecting money to acceptance, good behavior, and love.

( ) T ( ) F   11. Money was used to buy others' affections and make amends.

( ) T ( ) F   12. My parents were excessively restrictive with money—they counted every cent and had difficulty spending simply for pleasure.

( ) T ( ) F   13. I was not given guidelines about spending, saving, investing, and giving money.

( ) T ( ) F   14. I think the meaning and value of money was distorted in our family.

( ) T ( ) F   15. Money was used as a symbol for prestige and status in my community.

Fill in the blanks

My earliest money memory is   _____

_____.

The first money I ever earned was   _____

_____.

I remember saving my money for   _____

_____.

A time when my money was lost or stolen, I felt _____

_____.

What implicit messages did you receive about money?

_____

What feelings are provoked as you review your childhood associations with money? _____

_____

What patterns in your current money behavior can you connect with your childhood memories and experiences?

_____

How did your money behavior change as you entered puberty and adulthood, taking on a financial life of your own?

_____

What changes in your financial status occurred, and how did they affect the development of your money personality? ____

_____

From this exercise, can you see what early money memories have created the map with which you navigate your finances and life? What events and impressions have conspired to create your perspective of the financial terrain? Can you see how your money history is reflected in your current feelings and behaviors with finances? What parallels have you drawn? What feelings have been roused?

Remember, our money behaviors are not entirely rational—in fact, they rarely are. They are based on our learned responses to experiences. So whatever your habits with cold cash, cut yourself a break, knowing that at least some of what you do came from what you saw as you grew up.

Money and Meaning

We crave lives of meaning. We need to be affirmed and loved. That's why Jesse Jackson's rallying cry draws crowds as he urges them to proclaim: "I *am* somebody." We're all desperate to be somebody special. Buying, spending, and having money initially feed us with affirmation. We feel loved and pleased with ourselves. Perhaps your childhood memories include dialogue such as, "If you're a good girl while Mommy's gone, I will bring you a surprise," or, "If you get all As, you can have the Barbie-and-Midge-go-to-Tahoe set," or from Great-aunt Mildred, "You are so adorable in that fringed cowgirl dress." Were you offered money and stuff more frequently than verbal affirmation for good behavior?

Knowing how your money personality evolved is a key step toward gaining control and taking responsibility for the money part of your life. This will have a domino effect, reverberating positively into other areas of your life. Your money personality is not static. It changes as you gain or lose large amounts of money, gain maturity, or change perspective.

Money is scary. It's everything and everywhere. It creates fear, is difficult, is big, is important, knows all, creates happiness, causes problems, solves problems, creates conflict, unites enemies, and wreaks havoc.

My point is, if you've got some mess in your head about money, not to worry—you're in large company. Pretty much the rest of the universe is seeking love and true happiness, and many of your planet mates have been deceived into believing money is the road to finding it.

Does the pursuit of money drive your life? Truth be told,

money stresses me out. Money messes with my blood pressure, pulse rate, and body chemistry. Money is king. It has outpowered power; it rules and rocks. It is master of the universe. If money were a person, she'd be girlfriending with Oprah, sleeping in the Lincoln Bedroom, and noshing with the Pope.

Money is someone I don't trust. I don't trust her out with my friends. I don't feel comfortable letting her out of my sight. I think she should stay in and make demure. She should not be allowed to party nightly, engaging the crowd with her tantalizing talk and alluring gaze. I don't think she should drink, smoke, or brazenly flirt. She should sit on the bookshelf next to my encyclopedia set and keep quiet. Money is a flamenco dancer. She flaunts herself, seducing unsuspecting young boys. She takes their innocence before they know what hit them.

What is money for you? How does it behave for you? How does it smell, look, feel, sound, or itch? Is it friend or foe?

Personality Styles: What's Yours?

Perhaps in the following personality types, you'll recognize someone you know very well. You may not be able to change your basic personality type, but you can keep certain behaviors in check. Along with each type are some hints for overcoming the habits that make money a misery.

The Miser

Money came as spoilsport to the bash I attended in a multi-million-dollar penthouse overlooking Lake Michigan. The couple hosted a dinner party to celebrate their twenty-fifth wedding anniversary. The home was exquisite, the guests lovely, but money slid in, making a pouty appearance. Cheap food was consumed from paper plates. There were chips served out of the bag, processed meats and white buns, along with runny potato salad from the deli.

It seemed incongruent with the occasion but, more noticeably, the rest of this couple's lifestyle. They jetted internationally and dressed in the finest clothes. The dichotomy made the guests doubt how welcome they really were. You might think this couple had suddenly come into hard times, but they always entertained this way: spending generously on themselves, stingily on their guests.

Misers care about themselves, not others.

A remedy to this ailment is birthed from the Golden Rule: Treat others as you hope they would treat you. Show congruency both with yourself and across the social and economic strata— and don't treat your wealthy acquaintances differently than your poorer chums.

The Saving Hoarder

Terrified of daylight, people, and life itself, this money personality will not put its talents and skills to use. It has no interests, no social life, and doesn't even care for basic needs. She may live in a homeless shelter off the generosity of others, with no healthcare, warm coat, or place to call her own. There may be assets in a trust account, jewels in a vault, and stock and bond certificates stuffed inside the seat cushions, but little is spent to care for basic human needs. A spirit of scarcity and deprivation combined with disbelief in a God who cares about her needs leads to bizarre actions like sewing hundred-dollar bills in the lining of her frayed overcoat. In a world of desperate human need and limited resources, this sort of management is a sickness bordering on evil.

If you're afraid to spend, engage in a little behavioral therapy. Start small. Is it possible your lifestyle is painfully penurious in comparison to others at your level of resources? Buy new when something needs replacing. Make sure you're on schedule with medical, dental, and eye check-ups. Ensure that you're not shorting yourself on insurance coverage. And then, splurge on something you wouldn't normally buy for yourself. That's right—shop! If regret follows you home, consider whether it is false guilt nipping at the corners of your shopping bags. Consider the source of your sense of undeserving.

> Some people are making such thorough preparation for rainy days that they aren't enjoying today's sunshine.
>
> * William Feather *

The Spending Hoarder

A neighbor of mine was a Philippine lady in the end stages of cancer. As her hospice volunteer, I drove her around the neighborhood to do errands. One day, clutching a newspaper coupon, she asked me to take her to a kitchen supply store. We proceeded to pick out *six* identical glass teakettles and haul them to the checkout counter. I queried, ever so gently (I mean, she *was* terminally ill), "You sure you need *all* of these?"

Anything on sale she'd buy in bulk. I had difficulty getting inside her front door and was forced to turn and shuffle sideways down the front hall to her living room for all the stuff that lined the walls and was stacked, mountain-high, on the furniture. She no longer bathed in her bathtub—it had been filled with books and clothes, I suspect, years earlier. She slept in a recliner in the living room because her bedroom was so full of stuff she could not reach the bed. She was the Imelda Marcos of hoarders, except that she stashed a whole palace full of stuff into one Chicago flat.

She had once said her arranged marriage was miserable and her children were plain mean. Just a hip-pocket observation, but it seemed to me her accumulation of enough gadgets to fill two hardware stores was a sorry attempt to fill an empty heart. She thought that piles of stuff (ensuring you'd never run out of *any-thing* at all) could replace human relationship.

The hoarder that seeks to replace relationships with possessions ends up the loneliest of all.

Have you been accused of being a pack rat? Do you feel swamped with the stuff you've accumulated—can't close closet doors? Clean it out, give it away, and move somewhere else. Moving is one of the best instigators for discovering how much stuff you don't use or need. A forced purging will bring emotional and mental freedom like you can't imagine.

And stay out of stores. Buy only when you *need* it, not when you think you might need it later. For the hoarder: don't stock up, don't buy gifts months in advance (that ultimately stay in the closet for years), and give away everything of which you have duplicates. (Your coffee maker may last another five years, so give away the shiny new green one you got on clearance or bought at your neighbor's tag sale.)

The Greedy Accumulator

I can see them now, khaki-clad office workers shuffling two abreast on Wacker Drive, doing the nine-to-five. Although the shirts are no longer crisply white, but are now a bad knit-striped attempt at casual dress, their innards have not changed. They gripe, they moan, but on they go, prostituting their health, marriages, family, entire lives for the Holy Grail: the Almighty Dollar. Kissing up to people they despise, scheming to one-up their colleagues, they embellish expense accounts, lie about project results, don't deliver as promised, flush out a quick profit, and race cavalierly ahead to the next source of cash. In cahoots with their lawyers, accountants, and city hall, they disavow their own values. For what? Money.

Why are you in your job? Is it the right job for you, or the right job to amass cash? Most typically, do you enjoy the start of a workweek or workday? Why do you work? Assessing your skills and interests in a vocational-type exam or studying a few books on career development will help address these questions if you are dissatisfied with or unsure about your work life.

> Many men go fishing all of their lives without knowing that it is not a fish they are after.
>
> * Henry David Thoreau *

The Avoiding Perfectionist

When she thinks about financial planning, it brings on anxiety. She does not take responsibility for her money and avoids paying bills in a timely manner, choosing investments, and planning for tomorrow. She defers decision making to anybody else who might accept that role for her. She tosses credit card and ATM receipts and has little idea of her bank balances. She doesn't want to know, because she believes not knowing feels better than accepting the truth about her money. "Out of sight, out of mind" is her sorry motto.

She puts off investing because she's not going to do it until she has the time to investigate *all* possible alternatives and read the fourteen personal finance and investment books she's collected, as well as finally get to that stack of finance magazines.

If this describes you, start with something simple. Buy some nice file folders and dump in those receipts. Take it slowly. Next time a statement arrives, open it up and read it through. Commit to opening your mail the day it arrives. Gradually, like sticking a toe in the water and moving on up to your knees and thighs, you'll get used to it and slowly lose your distaste as you become accustomed to those little figures and columns marching across the page.

> Iron rusts from disuse; stagnant water loses its purity and in cold weather becomes frozen; even so does inaction sap the vigor of the mind.
>
> ✳ *Leonardo da Vinci* ✳

Procrastination is the perfectionist's nemesis. Get real. Money management is not an exact science, so there is not a single right way to do it. Don't think you're going to find it. If it's worth doing, it's worth doing badly, I say. You're going to have to make a decision sooner or later, so make one this week. Make an appointment with a financial adviser that a friend recommends, or read two articles on basic investing, and jump in the pool.

Start with a small purchase of an investment that appears prudent for you. You'll learn much more by getting involved and even making a few minor mistakes than by reading or observing. It's all in the doing.

The Love Seeker

This is the casual new friend of ordinary means who buys you an expensive birthday gift. She spends more than she can afford to get your friendship. Or it's the woman who just can't bring herself to date men who are not wealthy. Money and the gifts men buy her are an aphrodisiac. She'd choose to date money over personality or character. She feels special, loved, and respected when on the arm of a man who buys her fine baubles and takes her to the finest private clubs—no matter his actual reputation.

Graham notices that every time he's with a superwealthy friend of his, people they both know rush to greet the friend, ignoring him. Only when he is alone are those same people inclined to notice and approach him. Money buys attention, it buys lust, and it may even buy what poses as true love lasting for years; but it's only a veneer, not the real thing. Stormy days and the weathering of time will reveal what's underneath.

Don't give to get. And don't loiter around wealth, hoping to receive. If you lost all your money, which friends, do you suppose, would remain? If some of your wealthier friends lost all theirs, would you feel as devoted to them? Make a point of giving a little attention to the poorest friend at a party or in the church foyer. Spend no more for a gift for your wealthiest neighbor than for your poorest. (And the obvious: Don't date for dollars. It's been said that when you marry for money, you'll earn every cent.)

The Impulse Buyer

She spends when she sees it because when the need for a fix hits, she's got to gratify the wailing baby within. *Wait* is a four-letter word to this girl. A bit like the Avoiding Perfectionist, she doesn't consider her financial situation before making money decisions. That would cramp her style of buying beyond her means.

Nancy Reagan's solution is applicable here, if only it would work. Barring the ability to "just say no," work to create an environment conducive to making "no" easier. Turn off the TV, toss the magazines with glossy ads, stay out of the stores, and continue reading for more ideas on satisfying the compelling forces within.

The Peaceful Money Girl

She tends to her money and reviews her investments at regular intervals, but meantime, pays no mind to vagaries in the markets or the stuff her contemporaries are buying. She gives generously, pays bills and taxes in a timely manner, and has a sense that she has enough money and possessions to keep her content. She even splurges from time to time on herself and her friends.

Well, she's *good*. To her we'd say, "Just keep doing it and don't let your perfectness stand in contrast to our errant ways. But do give us an encouraging word or two." She's likely to be well-rounded in other areas of her life as well—physically fit, spiritually whole, and happy in relationship with family and friends. She may not always have been this way. She, too, is a work in progress and has been willing to learn from a variety of sources, including her own painful mistakes, observing others, and seeking out good information.

Don't be shy about asking her for a bit of advice. You'll surely have something to offer in return—like maybe showing her where to get the best coffee beans in town.

*   *   *

Wherever you find yourself with money, just remember what your coaches shouted at you in school. My most memorable phrase is one that, twenty-five years later, I can still hear my eight-months-pregnant basketball coach using after I'd bungled a play.

"Recover!" she'd scream from the sidelines, her belly heaving first to the left, then to the right.

When you make a mistake, immediately force it out of your head, get back into play, and focus on what's happening *now*. (You can always analyze your errors postgame, but never midplay.) Trust me on this: *Everyone* on the planet has made mistakes with their money. So just recover and get back in the game!

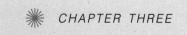

CHAPTER THREE

Know the Score

money and you

Answer true or false:

- I frequently argue with my spouse about money.
- I lose sleep at least once a week, thinking about my financial situation.
- I attribute much of my anxiety to my financial situation.
- I leave my bills unopened for days or weeks.
- I get depressed when I think about retirement.
- I get depressed when I see a lot of things I want but feel I cannot afford.
- I often find myself borrowing small items and money from others.
- I feel really far behind financially.

WHAT DO YOU KNOW ABOUT YOUR FINANCIAL STATUS? As my niece Nora would ask, "Where you is?" The first step is to map your current location. If you don't know where you is now and where you is going, you're sure to get there—nowhere. And it's not all about what comes in and what goes out. What stays in—the assets you accumulate and the status of their appreciation or depreciation—is also important to track. So many women say to me: "All I want to know is what I have, and how much I need."

To begin with, are your financial statements and records organized in a meaningful manner and readily accessible? Having your stuff in order is a huge component of financial success. It's easier to figure out where you are and what adjustments you need to make. I keep it simple: My statements are in separate manila file folders with the titles handwritten on the tabs. Consider keeping separate files and labeling them accordingly: credit card statements, mortgage statements, rental apartment leases, retirement accounts, money market funds, stock funds, and tax information, including receipts for charitable contributions and real-estate tax statements.

If you're not organized, start here. Take the time to sort your financial records into folders. You'll be glad you did.

Getting a clear picture of your financial scene is one way to break free of the emotions driving your money behaviors. With your emotions in the backseat, your reason and intellect take over, and your life can become a pleasant Sunday drive.

Joanna and Paul were afraid to look at their finances, feeling out of control and overwhelmed by debt. They were both nervous and subdued when they entered the coffee shop where we arranged to meet. It took us only an hour to review their assets and liabilities, creating a balance sheet using statements they had brought. They felt great relief in discovering the truth. Yes, their debt was huge, but their assets added up to much more than they'd thought. It was *good* news, and it gave them just the impetus to set up an aggressive debt reduction plan, making a not-bad financial situation better.

Discovering the facts of your finances can be so very freeing and affirming. Paying bills and getting your financial house in order is definitely clarifying and energizing. This energy spreads into other areas of your life where you feel out of control—your work life, dating life or marriage, spiritual life, physical fitness, and so on.

Money has such far-reaching effects. When Jesus said, "You cannot serve both God and Money,"[17] he was on to something big. It has always amazed me that Jesus did not say, "You cannot serve both God and your friends . . . or your sexual desires . . . or your career." He knew the weakest spot in most of us: the power of money. We can regain power over our money by taking some simple yet enormously important steps to ascertaining where we are.

Choose wisely when to organize. There's a time for getting the books in order and a time to let it wait another day (such as the Friday night after an exhausting week and a squabble with your spouse). But when you are unsure about your finances, going through the piled-up statements can be invigorating. It is empowering to reassert control—even if it's control over a messy financial situation. You'll feel recharged as you organize the fiscal chaos before you. It's like breaking out of a dust storm into the light of day. Once you can see the damage, you can get started on the cleanup. Knowing the ugly facts actually feels much better than continuing on with a nagging sense of the unknown.

Get a Financial Checkup

Here's a quick way to check up on the state of your fiscal health— what you have, what you owe, what your net worth is. (Net worth, a measure of your economic strength, is simply the total of your assets minus any debt.) Pull out your statements and complete the following personal financial statement. Do your best estimation where you don't have precise information, such as the current market value of your house or car. Better to take a shot at making a good guess than postpone doing this. Just pretend you're in the ER with some urgent symptoms—you're gushing blood or an arm bone is poking in the wrong direction—and don't put off checking those vital signs another minute.

The Current State of My Financial Affairs

Stuff I have—Assets:

$_____ Bank accounts—checking, savings, money market

funds, CDs, annuities

_____ Retirement and profit-sharing accounts—i.e., IRA, Roth IRA, 401(k), 403(b), Keogh, SEP, pension, profit sharing (include only fully vested amounts)

_____ Stocks

_____ Bonds

_____ Mutual funds

_____ Stock options

_____ Life insurance policies (cash value)

_____ Auto

_____ House, condo, other real estate (current value)

_____ Jewelry

_____ Art, antiques

_____ Boat, camper, outdoor equipment (cash value)

_____ Household furniture/possessions (cash value)

_____ Other

$_____ *Total*

Stuff I owe—Liabilities:

$_____ Mortgage

_____ Home equity loan

_____ Auto loan

_____ Education loans

_____ Credit card debt

_____ Additional secured or unsecured debt

_____ Other

$_____ *Total*

My assets less my liabilities = my fiscal net worth

$ _____ Total Assets

\- _____ Total Liabilities

= $ _____ Total Net Worth

Do know that having information, no matter how discomfiting, is a positive thing. Without it you'd be unable to find the signposts for the direction you want to go. Perhaps seeing your total assets listed was an encouraging surprise for you. If the results are discouraging, remember that financial assets are only a tiny component of who you are, and your identity should not be based on those numbers alone. Your real assets include your character, personality, skills, intelligence, and so forth.

Now that you've checked your basic vitals, if you wish to make a more thorough check of your symptoms and financial habits, see appendix A.

The good news is, you needn't revamp your life or even change all your poor fiscal habits. In fact, feel free to keep a few! Relax— perfection isn't attainable or even desirable. (If you were perfect, frankly, the rest of us couldn't stand to be around you for long anyway.) What you can do, however, is think about making a start for positive change. Replace a few habits with new behaviors brought on by thinking differently about money. If you take a step back and lapse into old behaviors, don't berate yourself—just start in again.

Embrace the reality of your financial situation. You can make lifestyle decisions that won't stretch your means or dampen your fun. Even one degree of movement changes your direction enough to take you to an entirely different destination. Imagine driving to California from Vermont. Ease into a turn outside of

Gary, Indiana, and you could find yourself wearing your flip-flops in Fargo.

Let's take the information you've gleaned and start immediately to boost your score.

The Number One Factor for Financial Success

A survey reported by *Microsoft Money* magazine uncovered what many Americans believe to be the keys to financial success. Responses included the ability to pick good investments, having a high-paying job, maintaining low debt, and marrying well.[18] Reading those survey results, I realized that more than two-thirds of the one thousand Americans polled did not know the most critical factor for achieving financial success.

> The greatest thing in this world is not so much where we are, but in what direction we are moving.
>
> * Oliver Wendell Holmes *

The answer? Having clearly defined goals.

Without goals, you've no context in which to navigate—you don't know whether you're hugging shore, treading in rocky waters, or heading out to the deep. Without goals, you'll have no idea how long it will take to get where you want to go. Without goals, you'll not know which direction to turn and what choices to make. Most critically, you won't recognize financial success when you see it.

What is financial success anyway? Financial success, according to my wise friend Jeanie, who has personally known poverty *and* wealth, is this: being content with what you have. That being true, financial success is not a constant for all. It has more to do with the head and the heart and less with the wallet and the balance sheet. So get some goals so you can get some financial success, as you define it!

Before you set out to have a million dollars by next year, you must know what it is that, deep down in your heart, will bring true satisfaction. Before you create goals, you must be in touch with yourself enough to know what will make you happy and satisfied. Unless you know what is important to your happiness, you can forget marking out a goal to get there. Thus, the first step to achieving financial success is knowing your values, knowing what is meaningful to you.

There is danger in setting goals without thought to values. Some people work all their lives only to discover they've hit targets their neighbor set. And what's worse—they don't even *like* that neighbor.

Goals Rise from Values

Determine what financial priorities fall naturally out of your key values. What is most meaningful to you about having financial resources? Put differently, what do you need for your happiness and physical, mental, emotional, and spiritual survival? What do you most value that money can help you achieve?

Your response to these questions will help determine whether your values and money behaviors are in alignment. When life values and money behavior are incongruous, huge amounts of energy are required to manage the tension that inevitably ensues. Thus "money angst"—stress from guilt and fear—will rob us of joy and life itself.

From a highly narrow sampling (my coffee-shop poll), my friends and one stranger had this to say:

What's Important about Having Money

Dana, actor and model: "The ability to travel, to discover how I interact and become different with different cultures. Also, the freedom to do my creative projects which connect me with myself."

Maribeth, homemaker and former commodities trader: "It brings me freedom of choice and options, and how I spend my time."

Lisa, factory worker: "The ability to pay my bills and not have creditors making those harassing calls."

Ron, retiree (sans front teeth): "I need it to survive."

What's important to you about having money?

If your answer is *security,* then ask—what does security look like? Is it money in the bank, just enough to keep you under a roof, enough to cover health and long-term care insurance, to keep creditors at bay, a nest egg to carry you through a year of unemployment?

If money means *independence* to you, does that mean the ability to support yourself, to have enough money to live alone and care for your basic needs, or to keep you in fine luxuries? Remember, nobody's an island, and people who have thought they were include the likes of Ted Kaczynski. Even Henry David Thoreau wasn't on Walden's Pond forever.

If money means *freedom,* does that mean freedom to live anywhere, travel frequently, take a job regardless of compensation level, or to be your own boss? Remember, freedom without responsibility ultimately collapses into entropy or licentiousness. *That* can't be good.

If *peace of mind,* what is that for you? Can money buy sanity? Ask the late Howard Hughes—or rather, his caretakers.

Where would you like to be in five years? Who would you like to be in five years? What would you like to be in five years? Jot down some personal values. Then we'll move into making those into tangible goals.

My Values

_____

_____

_____

_____

_____

From Values to Goals

Goals must be something you really want, not something you think you should want. They should be personal, tailored to what you believe will give you satisfaction. That's why identifying your values—what you know brings you contentment and fulfillment—is so important.

In the Sydney, Australia, summer games, Marion Jones became

> Watch your thoughts; they become words.
> Watch your words; they become actions.
>   Watch your actions; they become habits.
>   Watch your habits; they become character.
>   Watch your character; it becomes your destiny.
>
> ✳ *Frank Outlaw* ✳

the first woman in Olympic history to win five medals in track-and-field events. When she was eight years old, she had written on a blackboard in her bedroom, "I want to be an Olympic champion."[19] Get out your own chalk because, as George Eliot said, "It is never too late to be what you might have been."

First review your key values to determine what goals will help get you there. Perhaps you wrote independence, peace of mind, time with family, health, or your relationship with God. Long-term goals reflecting those values might include your education, your children's education, preservation of assets for heirs, retirement by a specific age and a specific level of assets, insurance for medical and long-term care expense, a house or a second home, or a specific sum contributed to charities. Short- or mid-term goals might include paying off debt, purchasing a car or house, earning a college degree, or taking your parents to Spain.

Following are the keys for establishing goals that work for you.

Be Specific

Remember what your coaches (except the swimming one) shouted to you: "Rufus, keep your eye on that ball!" Write, "I'll pay off all my unsecured debt" or "I'll invest in a stock mutual fund." Instead of a stated goal of "I'll be more generous," state, "I'll give $500 to a charity."

Make It Measurable

For example, "I'll pay an additional $150 toward my credit card balance each month." "I will arrange for direct deposit of four percent of each paycheck into a mutual fund." "I'll give $50 every month for two years to XYZ mission."

Set a Timeline

Establish an end date by which you will achieve the goal. Map a timeline of secondary goals en route to the final goal. "I'll pay off all unsecured debt in the next eighteen months." "I'll save enough money in the next three months to make the minimum purchase required in a stock mutual fund." "I'll give $500 to XYZ charity over the next three months."

Make It Realistic

But don't make it falling-out-of-your-wallet easy. Stretch a bit. If you don't set some fantastic goals, well, it stands that you may not do some fantastic things. Set a goal that's challenging but not impossible to achieve. Look over your spending patterns to determine whether it is possible to pay an additional $100 per month toward debt reduction. If it looks easily achievable, ratchet it up a notch to $200 or $300. For our Rockefeller readers, you might make that $2,000 to $3,000. Squeeze just enough to make it feel a little bit good, but not so tight that you can't breathe comfortably.

Document Your Goal

Write the goal on an index card and keep it in a place where you'll see it daily, such as on your dressing room door or car dashboard, or input it as your mobile phone welcome message. My mom puts hers on the window sill over the kitchen sink. I tape mine inside my closet door and sometimes on the bathroom wall. If you don't write it down in black and white, it doesn't exist, and it will disappear like a fog when the sun rises.

Write down your goals in these boxes. Make them come alive in black and white.

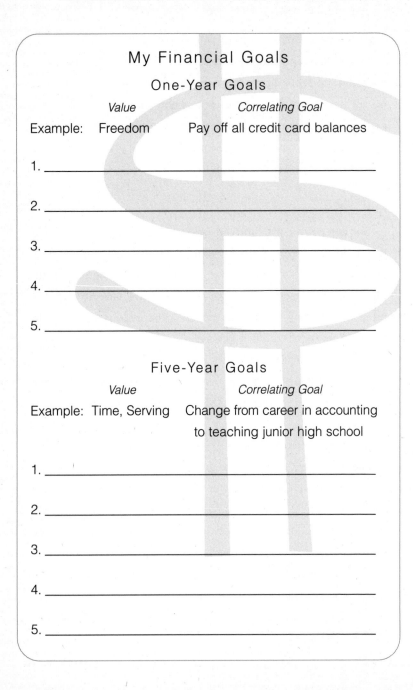

My Financial Goals

One-Year Goals

	Value	*Correlating Goal*
Example:	Freedom	Pay off all credit card balances

1. _____

2. _____

3. _____

4. _____

5. _____

Five-Year Goals

	Value	*Correlating Goal*
Example:	Time, Serving	Change from career in accounting to teaching junior high school

1. _____

2. _____

3. _____

4. _____

5. _____

You Are on Your Way!

Financial columnist Humberto Cruz suggests tallying your financial statement once a year. He does it on his birthday. I update the current value of my assets in Excel as statements arrive throughout the month, but retain a record to compare net assets year over year as of December 31.

You can't move successfully toward a destination without knowing where you are; you can't travel meaningfully without a map. By getting a financial checkup, evaluating the values closest to your heart, and building goals based on that information, you have set foot on the road to financial freedom. Remember what motivational speakers often pontificate: If you fail to plan, you plan to fail. Knowing you are executing a plan will keep you on track and motivate you to further financial success. Congratulations, you've hit the road running!

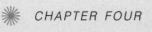
Diets Don't Work and Neither Do Budgets

money and you

Take a moment to consider:

- Is your current lifestyle one you consciously chose?
- In the last six months, what financial lifestyle decision(s) have you made (i.e., change in job or living situation, a large purchase, joining a social club, etc.)?
- Has your lifestyle inflated over time? Did this happen gradually or sharply?
- How have lifestyle changes affected your happiness quotient?
- At what checkpoints could you stop to make decisions about decelerating upward float—the subtle, gentle rise in the level of things you require?
- Are you satisfied with the time your current lifestyle affords for rest and relaxation?
- Does your lifestyle give you enough margin for the levels of giving and saving you want?
- Would your lifestyle be at significant risk if you were to have no income for six months (due to debilitating illness or other unexpected occurrence)?

HAVE YOU EVER OPENED YOUR WALLET ONLY TO discover that a thief has offed with your cash, leaving only a few wrinkled George Washingtons? Are there frequent mass dollar migrations out of your wallet? Do these thefts typically occur shortly after a weekend of running errands? No one opens her purse and says, "Where did all that money come from?!" More often we hear ourselves shriek, "There's no way I spent that much!"

When we spend, it's like Delilah trimming Samson's hair, such is the loss of potency. What is the Delilah in your life, sapping your economic strength and solvency by robbing you of the money you've saved and grown over time? Your capital resources, freedom, and energy seep away. You think they're simply unnoticed pennies, but like single drops of water, they cumulate to form a torrential flood eroding your net worth. A television ad for Citibank proclaimed: "Live richly. Just because you have the power doesn't mean you should use it all up." To live richly, spend wisely. Save your bullets. Choose your battles. Choose your expenditures and don't fall for the quick exhilarating hit that leaves you in a weakened stupor.

Let's be clear: Budgets are not the answer to controlling your spending. Diets—including financial ones—don't work. Lifestyle changes do work, and *how!* Small changes create or effect large changes. Action breeds action. Constraints only serve to make us grumpy. Tonia and Matt spent hours constructing a budget each year, but she confessed, "It was all a lie. We would say our electricity costs were $40 a month, but the electricity was *never* $40. We just didn't want to set aside money for something as dull as utilities. We were lying to ourselves so we could have more fun. The big lie was groceries. The last thing you want to say is, 'When we get a raise, we'll up the mundane food budget.'"

> A budget is simply a method of worrying before you spend money.
>
> ✳ *unknown* ✳

Lifestyle changes are effected by eliminating the lies and replacing them with the truth. Change what you believe and you change your behavior.

I'm going to break rank and confess that I have never created or used a written budget. Perhaps my resistance to budgets has to do with how I react to imposed restrictions. I am better motivated by positive input. Because I am good at math and have an excellent memory for numbers, I've usually had an accurate grasp on what money I've got and what expenses and bills are forthcoming. Diets don't work for me because they cause me to focus on food I can't have. A budget would cause me to react similarly: I would think of all the things I should not buy.

I've found that a woman without a budget—but with a financially responsible lifestyle—does not feel constricted or deprived, because she has no limits. She maintains her spending below her earnings and knows where those numbers are. Living below her means lets her feel very free. She has a cushion of money so that when she sees something she really wants, she doesn't feel constrained in buying it. This way, she has control over how and what she spends and rarely experiences the guilt of poor spending choices. It's all a matter of balance: We should be conscious of what we eat and conscious of what we spend. We shouldn't fixate on either.

To budget or not to budget. The key is really to adopt a moneyed lifestyle that helps you live and interact positively with your cash flow. Self-discipline, resourcefulness, and self-awareness are some of the amazing things you'll discover anew in your journey to an authentic lifestyle—toward sensible, controlled (not controlling), frugal, and best of all, abundant living.

Work It Out, Baby

If you think you have money problems, brew yourself a cup of tea, sit down with pen and paper, and work to define them—to pinpoint and best articulate the real problems behind the apparent ones. Dig down. Write. Think. Sip. Write some more. It will come.

Oh, honey, if we could just hear the truth. But over the bleating, screeching, honking, and shrieking of Wall Street, Main Street, and Madison Avenue, I concede: It's difficult to hear. So get quiet. You will discover that your money problems arise from lifestyle problems, and these are what you must identify. Let the questions at the beginning of the chapter guide your examination. List what you know is actually draining your checkbook dry.

It's been said you are well on your way to a solution if you can understand the problem. Consultants will tell you that defining the problem is difficult; recommending and/or implementing solutions is the easy part.

Once you've discovered where your lifestyle has expanded beyond your means, determine to set about fixing it. Get real. Your money problems will not disappear on their own—not with your next pay raise, bonus, birthday cash, wealthy fiancé, second weekend job, and most certainly not through a lottery ticket. A change in what you believe to be true about money, which, in turn, impacts the way you live, is the answer.

Warning: As you seek a new life and, thus, a new financial status, beware the temptation to establish a lifestyle based on what you can afford. "Huh?" you may ask. Research indicates that, regardless of income level, Americans are increasingly spending beyond their means.[20] If you set your lifestyle to the level of income you hope to achieve, then you put serious restrictions on your life and future. You bind, tie, and handcuff yourself. By living flush with what you can financially pull off, you are, effectually, playing God. You have committed yourself to the rat race, eliminating options for your future happiness such as volunteerism, charity, travel, retiring sooner, time to heal from an injury or to nurse a sick family member, or perhaps opting for a career you love more that might pay less. Lily Tomlin told us the problem with winning the rat race is that when it's over, you're still a rat. Don't automatically allow money to be the key determinant when making important life decisions.

Watch Your Money Language

Never say, "I can't afford it." This implies that you would normally spend all the money you have, and the only reason you aren't buying is because you are completely broke. Watch your money language. Better to speak from a position of strength: "I choose not to spend my money this way because this thing is not a priority now, or maybe ever." Eradicate negative thoughts and words that create a mentality of deprivation. I actually feel I can afford nearly everything that I want. No, I'm far from rich, but I feel prosperous because I simply don't allow my wants to wander off, deviating far from my financial ability to fill them. Because I can buy more than I actually do, I'm more inclined to demur and think, "I don't really want that." And I don't, because in the buying I'd lose my freedom to buy something else—say a pickup truck with matching cowboy boots or, more likely, a retirement before four score and seven years have passed me by.

Make better choices. You'll find that embarking upon the positive lifestyle change of living below your means can feel like a grand adventure. Because you know the result will be your emotional liberty and financial health, it's almost easy. The relief alone of having a plan of action will give you immense energy and renewed motivation, and a fresh start can give you enough wherewithal to endure when the going gets tough.

The following pages contain ideas to help you develop your own money lifestyle. Choose those that will work best for your

An American tourist visited the nineteeth-century Polish rabbi Hofetz Chaim. Astonished to see the rabbi's room was only a simple room, filled with books, plus a table and a bench, the tourist asked, "Rabbi, where is your furniture?"

"Where is yours?" replied the rabbi.

"Mine?" asked the puzzled American. "But I'm a visitor here. I'm only passing through."

"So am I," replied Rabbi Chaim.

personality and temperament—no more than three to start—and begin to implement them.

When you've a new idea, you must do one thing within the next day toward implementing it. After that twenty-four-hour window, the odds drop significantly that you'll take action and follow through. That one thing could be making an appointment, looking up information, phoning one friend for a referral, or retrieving a file to research your financial information. Act quickly. Build momentum. Create speed. You'll see.

A Money Lifestyle That Promises Abundance—Little Steps for Big Change

Home

Spend money to save money. Are your worn appliances inefficient? Maintenance and repair—fixing the washing machine rattle when it first occurs, for instance—are typically much cheaper than replacement costs.

Avoid waste. Do you have exercise equipment used solely as a clothes rack? Have you left a tool outdoors to rust? What's in your closet with the tags still attached? Turn the hot water heater down a notch when the house isn't full of sweaty people in need of showers. Crank the furnace and air conditioning down if you're out all day.

Switch to basic or no cable. I daresay you might enjoy your life more without it. I catch up on *Larry King Live* when staying in hotels. Mind you, if cable is really important to you and going without it is your definition of asceticism, then subscribe! The point is, most of you would probably live just as happily without it, so give it a try.

Rent out a room, or downsize to a smaller but equally nice home.
Debbie Dunnewold resigned her position with a global consulting
firm to start a personal chef business. While getting her business
off the ground, she took in a roommate, a trusted friend whose
rent helped make the mortgage payments on her two-bedroom
city condo.

Health

Keep health checkups current to save money (and yourself) in the
long run. One of the most costly and unexpected drains on your
finances can be medical expenses.

Maintain your health. Floss, fasten your seat belt, eat raw veggies by the bushel, exercise like an unleashed puppy, avoid bad
stuff—you know the drill.

Personal Services

Do it yourself: the manicure, oil change, taxes, skirt hem, bicycle
tune-up, deck refinishing. Many dry-cleanable fabrics are hand-
washable. It feels so good to do some things for yourself.

Review costly services. I have seen beautiful haircuts on women
only to discover they go to Cuts-R-Us. Are you truly getting the
best value from Jean Pierré Michele Francois Devéreaux's spa
cuts, with "free" espresso, neck massage, and forty-dollar blow-
dry? Get an expensive haircut one month, then follow up with a
few cheaper ones.

Space your services. If you're just a little bit of a diva, but you've
found your finances tightening, schedule your personal services
farther apart. Get your hair coloring and styling, massage, manicure, dog grooming, and housecleaning done, say, every six weeks
instead of four. That's less painful than forgoing them altogether.

Wear it out. Use it up. Keep the new sneakers in the back of the closet until you wear out the old ones. My mother rotated her Sunday dresses down to everyday wear, and cycled the everyday dresses to work dresses. Actually use up all those cosmetic samples cluttering your cabinets before buying more.

> Wisdom begins with sacrifice of immediate pleasures for long-range purposes.
>
> ✳ *Louis Finkelstein* ✳

Mind travel expenses. Skip in-flight headphones for the magazine, and wine for water. So you're a water connoisseur? Bring the bottle of water you bought at Sam's Club instead of buying one at the airport shop for three dollars more. Because airline meals have all but disappeared, I'm never without a protein bar and an apple in my pack, so as not to hit a sugar low when waiting for hours on the tarmac for a loose screw to be tightened. It tastes better than the soggy ten-dollar turkey sandwich you grabbed in the terminal.

Cancel the private driver and take a taxi. You don't have a chauffeur? Skip the taxi and take a bus. Or save bus fare and walk. When I was a stockbroker's assistant, I walked three miles round-trip to work every day. My manager thought I was a little nuts until I pointed out an annual savings of $500—not an insignificant portion of my $14,400 annual income. It also eliminated health-club fees. Although my income later soared, I bicycled eight miles to work during the summers I was a VP and broker, because I felt so great by the time I started work at 7:00 A.M.

Choose your own give-ups: sodas and vending-machine snacks, newspapers at the stand rather than a subscription, weekly movies with all the concession snacks. What are the little leaks putting your ability to stay afloat at risk?

Financial Management

Get insured. Just one financial catastrophe has put people in homeless shelters. Don't skimp here. Even a small loss can badly gouge your nice money plan.

Increase insurance deductibles. Even if you make a claim and pay the larger deductible, over time you will spend significantly less. It's critical to insure for catastrophic loss, but it's prudent to self-insure for smaller losses. It might help you to set aside the difference you save in lower premiums to cover the larger deductible.

Pay dues, fees, and subscriptions annually or biannually for discounted rates.

Establish automatic deposits to investment or savings accounts from your paycheck, when possible. Establish 401(k), 403(b), a medical savings account, and other pretax withdrawal options. The less you have, the less you'll spend. What you can't see, you won't miss.

Don't squander new money. Direct "found" money toward debt first, or else save and invest it. (Every bonus I have ever received went directly into an investment account. I don't think of it again. This includes the thousand dollars I received for my tenth anniversary at Fuji Securities. When I treat myself, it's from my regular earnings.)

Homeowners, refinance your mortgage and appeal your property tax assessment. Doing both saved me a few thousand dollars in 2001 alone.

Club dues. Drop the luxe health club and join the YMCA if you don't use your club primarily for socializing or scouting for dates.

Avoid unnecessary fees. Use credit cards with no annual fees. Get free banking services. I have never paid one cent in checking fees, and you shouldn't either. Ask. Don't be surprised when you call service companies to ask them to eliminate fees and they readily agree.

Never miss a payment. If you only miss one, call and ask for the late fee to be dropped.

Arrange for utility bills (gas, electric, phone) to be automatically deducted from your bank accounts. Do not automatically deduct discretionary items; you will be more likely to take note of and reconsider those expenses—such as your cable bill or health club memberships—when you physically scratch out the check each month.

Negotiate everywhere. Always ask car-rental agencies and hotels for discounts. You might get one because you are a AAA member, a frequent flier, because it's Tuesday, or your name starts with the letter W. I once upgraded to a convertible for a weekend in San Diego at no extra charge when I offered the desk clerk a stick of gum. Ask a boutique owner for a volume discount or to throw in a free item with your purchases. This especially works at consignment shops. Their goal is turnover, and you can help them do that.

Food

Buy the finest coffee beans. Just brew 'em at home for a chubby savings over coffee-to-go.

Cook it yourself. It's healthier and fresher; you'll lose weight and be less likely to get a local version of Montezuma's revenge. Fill your grocery cart with more fresh fruits and vegetables and fewer processed items that come in boxes, foil bags, cellophane packaging, and glass jars—you know, the ones with the big markups.

Replace soda with water. You'll probably live longer too without the sugar, caffeine, or sweetener substitutes. Have you the mindset of Jeff Rogers, who will drink only Coke and Pepsi? "I don't drink water," he says. "That stuff falls from the sky."[21] Stuff that's free or nearly so gets no respect.

Quit going gourmet. If you stopped buying coffee-to-go ("take-away" if you live in Manhattan), over twenty-five years, invested monthly, assuming a 10 percent return, you'd have savings of $63,688.[22] Some financial experts refer to it as the latte factor. Don't stop at coffee. (And go ahead and get the Venti™ latte if forgoing it altogether would truly be a sacrifice.)

Stuff

Put more effort and less money into wedding, birthday, and baby gifts. I made a thank-you gift that was a book of photos and writings with exquisite handmade paper, leaves, and flowers, adorned with luscious ribbons that I purchased at a stationer's—inexpensive, but rich with love and care.

Skip Christmas gifting. Who says you can't? Author Bill McKibben questions the paradox of "whether we should celebrate the birth of a man who said we should give all that we have to the poor by showering each other with motorized tie racks. . . . All that wrapping paper, all those batteries."[23] Christmas has evolved into an excuse for the ultimate shopping orgy. "Christmas is like the Super Bowl of bad financial decisions," write two authors on debt elimination.[24] If you do gift, put more effort and less money into it.

Anticipate. Buy it before you need it. Convenience stores are just that: convenient for the bank accounts of its owners, pocketing hefty profits because you are too lazy to get yourself to the grocer or warehouse store on time. Buy gifts in advance of the party, because last-minute purchases are rarely cheap.

Mail packages early, using third or fourth class. By being frugal with the shipping mode, you can be more generous in the giving. I once sent a birthday gift a few weeks early. My postmaster laughed at my choice of shipping class, until I said, "Well, would you leave a couple of dollars lying on the sidewalk?"

Take care of your stuff. Take that car in for an oil change. Check the tires. (Seriously, lots of people don't actually do this.)

Keep your car. The cheapest car you can drive is the one you currently own. Don't replace it until you absolutely must.

Divorce your car. "Divorcing your car can take many forms, from simply using it less to not owning one at all."[25] Remeet your feet, board a bike, take a train, hop a bus, and lower your stress level.

Carpool. In some cities, you get the carpool lane where you can speed right past those annoying traffic backups, saving time and money.

Never buy a lottery ticket. Tell me you don't know the odds are just as good that you'll discover a million-dollar bearer bond stuck in the library book you checked out last week.

Drop off your clothes at a consignment store for extra cash. They typically split the amount of the sale with you. Stores prefer fashionable items that are seasonable. (Don't bring your winter coat in June.)

Find cheap entertainment. It's probably more fun. Camp in a state park, go to the community swimming pool (get to know your neighbors), rent movies and books on tape or get them from the library for free, jog, bike, and play football in the park. Attend free outdoor concerts in your neighborhood. Usher at the local theater to see the performances free. Tour the museum on the free day.

Create your own list. I don't have the corner on ideas for capital preservation. You know yourself. I've listed a few tactics primarily to stimulate your finely tuned brain to dream up its own creative, realistic, and fun solutions to root out wasteful or needless spending and establish a healthier money lifestyle. You bright-eyed material mongers will discover ideas hiding in plain sight, once you adjust your lenses ever so slightly.

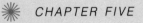 *CHAPTER FIVE*

Chemo for Debt I:
Diagnosis and Treatment

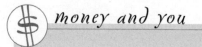 *money and you*

Take a moment to consider:

- Do you cringe when the phone rings, fearing it's another creditor calling?
- Do you argue with your spouse over bills?
- Has your debt caused you to lie or cheat?
- Do you consistently make late payments on your bills?
- Do you suspect you're living a more luxurious lifestyle than befits your income?
- Do you know the difference between prudent borrowing and foolish borrowing?
- Is debt beginning to affect different areas of your life? Is it impacting your moods, energy, and relationships?
- Do you know exactly how much debt you have?

SOME PEOPLE SAY *DEBT* IS A FOUR-LETTER WORD. It's not. Well, it is, but you get what I mean. Debt, in and of itself, isn't a bad thing. How you treat debt has everything to do with how debt will treat you. There are some critical things to know: the different kinds of debt, how to use debt to your advantage, and—most importantly—how to avoid and/or dig yourself out from expensive and unnecessary debt. (It's like escaping a manipulative, abusive relationship: First, you recognize it for what it is; next, you find support to help extricate yourself from it; and last, you get involved in a good, healthy, loving relationship.)

When used well, debt can be a valuable tool to flourishing economically. (For many, it's successfully used to gain asset appreciation via home ownership or to build a business.) When debt is mismanaged, it's typically for one of two reasons: lack of good information and understanding about debt, and lack of control over spending in the hopes of satiating our rapacious desires. The good news is, there is treatment for the disease of debt.

Eradicate Debt Ignorance

First, you've got to have a clear understanding of your own debt picture. The secret to victory over debt is information, information, information. This is your first and critical line of defense. You must know what kind of debt and how much debt you have, as well as what that debt costs you financially and emotionally.

With that critical data in hand, you can determine whether your debt is appropriate for you. For example, does it cost you more than you're earning on savings accounts or other investments? (If you have a savings account in which you are earning, say, 1.5 percent in interest and also have a credit card balance at one of those introductory low rates of, say, 6.9 percent, then you are paying about 5.4 percent too much.) Is it manageable, or do you have too much of it relative to your needs, income, and assets? Is it sapping your energy and straining your resources? What do you see as your financial and emotional ability to repay that debt?

You can create a personalized chemotherapy to help you escape the dark valley of the shadow of debt. There *is* hope out of the crushing entrapment you may feel. While there are questions I cannot answer, I can show you ways to gain victory over the bad debt in your life.

First, let's differentiate between types of debt.

Debt: The Good and the Bad

Good debt and bad debt are fairly explicit.

Good debt is debt for which you have an underlying appreciating asset. That would include student loans, because education is an asset that builds your skills and employability, increasing your productivity. Good debt also includes debt on appreciable property, such as real estate.

Good debt is debt you can economically justify—you can repay it when it is due. It fits within your spending plan. It is debt for which you have planned and studied, and that you have entered into with all the information available to you, using your most prudent judgment, and with an eye to reality.

Good debt is debt you can pay based on your current finances, *not* money you anticipate getting. Until you see the whites of George Washington's eyes, it isn't yours.

Good debt is debt that doesn't hold life's opportunities ransom. It doesn't keep your hands tied. Good debt doesn't limit your options. You don't tie up future earnings to make the debt affordable today. As I wrote the check for my modest new car, the dealer told me he'd underwritten car loans for terms up to eight years. Tying up your resources is not a wise move. Such debt will inhibit you from following your dreams, which you have just forced to a higher price point.

Good debt (for me) is my mortgage, low enough to fit within my expected earnings. You may determine after much investigation and introspection that taking on debt to start a business is a wise choice. Good debt is an investment in your future when it is leveraging an asset that increases your productivity or your personal or professional value, when it enhances your ability to earn a living or contribute positively to your lifework.

Bad debt is simply the converse of good debt. It hasn't been thought through. It strains your finances *and* your blood pressure. It's debt that can't be paid off in a timely manner. It's unsecured debt for things you've bought that plummet in value the minute you scrawl your John Hancock and sashay out of the store with it or *vroom* off the lot.

Bad debt is buying stuff on credit solely to rack up frequent flier miles, and getting caught paying interest on the unpaid balances.

Bad debt is debt for a new car when you should continue to drive the old one. (You should keep driving the old one if a new car loan and insurance payments would be a financial strain and the old one is still safe to drive.)

> Never spend your money
> before you have it.
>
> ✶ *Thomas Jefferson* ✶

Bad debt is debt for things you don't really need—particularly if the spending causes friction in your family, liabilities on your ledger, or distress in your dreams.

Bad debt is any debt you don't understand or isn't useful and productive. It's debt you don't know how you'll pay back. It is debt that you pay off by floating checks or taking a cash advance from another credit card account.

Bad debt is unessential debt undertaken for depreciating assets, such as the sailboat you can only use three months of the year on Lake Michigan. (There's absolutely nothing wrong with having a sailboat; it's simply relative: If it fits easily within your financial capabilities, by all means, go sail!)

Bad debt ties up your money and, thus, your opportunities. My aunt and uncle, retired missionaries in their early seventies, had settled in a Michigan farmhouse, loving the proximity to their grandchildren and our family's 106-year-old matriarch. When they received a call offering a job in northeastern Russia, they responded excitedly, unafraid to board an aging former Aeroflot jet. They abandoned comfy retirement for hard linguistic labor, teaching ESL at a Communist-youth-camp-turned-Bible institute.

Because they were missionaries who had not retired rich, I just assumed they needed the extra income, until I discovered they wouldn't be paid so much as a ruble. It gets better—or worse. The institute couldn't pay for their excursion to that frigid, foreign, forsaken tundra. They could have gotten a few runs to Hawaii and back for less than the cost of their flight from Detroit to Petropavlovsk-Kamchatskiy, not a frequently traveled route.

But they were thrilled to go. They even paid their own room and board. The job roused them and was, as they said, an incredibly rewarding culmination of their lifelong mission. They're grateful they did not have immense debt that would have prohibited them from taking this life-affirming work.

If you tie up your money, you won't be able to grab opportunities as they arise. You just might miss out on the most rewarding adventure of your livelong life—and perhaps yours will be on a tropical isle, not a Siberian work camp. Don't keep yourself so far in hock that you aren't free to take a thrilling, but possibly lower paying job next month, or join the Peace Corps in your later years for the time of your life. You've only got one life. Don't let slavery to debt rob you of your future.

Is your credit card balance increasing or decreasing each month? Are you paying interest on purchases such as groceries, medical bills, and other necessities? If so, you're on debt overload. If you have undertaken debt as a temporary measure because of a financial emergency of sorts (a new boat doesn't count), and you have a plan to pay it off as soon as possible, I would call that appropriate debt.

The Economy of You

Next, let's talk about you. Where is your debt? Imagine receiving your interest payments as bills separate from your credit card purchases. What would those numbers look like? How much do you think it adds up to at the end of the year? What concrete value do you get from paying those interest rates—the ability to buy four new sweaters this season instead of two? Is it worth it?

Let's mine the facts. Be strong; you can do this. If you so much as suspect debt trouble brewing yonder, we'd best find out where you are, so we can map out where to go.

Pull your credit statements out of the drawer and detail the following information for each account in separate columns: name of the creditor, balance, minimum payment due, and interest rate. Total the balances and the minimum payments due.

How does the total balance due compare with your monthly aftertax income? How much of a bite are the interest payments taking from your "fun" (discretionary) money? Optimal numbers are balances that you can readily pay in full each month with your discretionary income, so as to incur no interest payments.

For example, our fictional friend Minerva has the following credit card accounts:

Creditor	Balance	Minimum due	Interest rate
Sears	$502.43	$ 20.00	12.40%
MasterCard	877.86	17.00	14.65
Shell	131.03	10.00	19.74
Visa	1,490.49	31.00	15.40
Total	$3,001.81	$78.00	

OK. Perhaps you've decided that you just might be on debt overload. What to do? Follow the directive of my favorite phrase that has brought peace of mind to so many areas of my life: Do what you can do, not what you can't.

Overcoming Debt

OK, deep breath. First, show up at the starting gate. It can be done, perhaps faster than you think, and without severe pain. You may be surprised at how much you enjoy it. You'll be propelled forward by the ensuing satisfaction, building a sweet momentum toward success. Starting is the hardest part. So just start.

Second, get honest. Commit to the truth. If you've overindulged for years with abandon, just say it, out loud. Admit it to your spouse, to your best friend.

Third, establish a plan. The plan you will create is two-pronged. You'll create a payoff plan that works with your income and your personality to eradicate debt. You'll also develop a spending strategy that ensures you don't take on new debt and can make regular payments toward paying down debt. If you have a goal, if you have a payoff plan, it can be so very easy to hit the bull's-eye.

Fourth, get happy. Learn the joy of simpler living and relish the freedom that comes from eradicating money anxiety.

Become Your Own Private Eye

You cannot formulate a payoff plan or spending strategy without reviewing your monthly income and outflow. Income would be wages, investment income, child support, cash from a moonlighting gig, etc.

Then you'll need to go one step further: Find out exactly where all your money goes. This is an extremely simple but monumental task. I suggest you carry a pocket-sized spiral-bound notebook. Write down every cent you spend. I'll be honest: I have found this to be the most difficult discipline to undertake—next to eliminating sugar and caffeine. See appendix B for an income and spending worksheet you may use to more easily compile, tabulate, and review your findings.

Without knowing what sieve your cash flows through, you cannot stave off increasing debt or pay off your account balances. Like a heat-seeking missile, track the whereabouts of every cent, every expenditure.

My expenditures for one Wednesday in September:
- $3.35 – greeting cards
- 7.75 – vegetables at farmer's market
- 0.75 – five copies at the printer's
- 36.38 – groceries
- 14.14 – used book purchased on-line
- $62.37 – Total

Itemize in categories that are relevant to you and total those categories at the end of the month. Do this for at least one month. It helps to retain receipts until you've documented the purchase. It's essential to check at the end of every day to be sure you've tracked it all. It helps to corral your spouse or a friend to do it with you in a show of solidarity. It helps to keep the notebook with your wallet or in your calendar. Use a PDA if you're so inclined.

This practice will give you an acute awareness of the amount and destination of the money flowing through your fingers. How much, how often, what for, and what you're feeling when it's happening. You will find some surprises. I found two—food and clothes. I spent amazing amounts of money on restaurants and takeaway meals. I've always said I was a low-maintenance kind of girl and didn't think I bought *that* many new clothes. Well, clotheshorse I am, with the receipts to prove it.

Your raised shopping consciousness will serve as a motivation to spend more efficiently and prudently. That information alone will act as a natural appetite suppressant.

The second thing your little notebook can help you determine is exactly *where* you can carve out the additional money you need to commit toward your credit card balance. Stick to paying your fixed expenses, necessities, and the sum you elected to pay toward the credit card balances first. Live on what is left over. Once your debt is paid off, put that same sum into savings and investments.

Remember, if holding a finger in the dike will prevent the village from flooding, if securing little-bitty screws in place will prevent the jetliner from crashing—trust me on this—tracking your money with a little-bitty notebook can prevent you from financial failure. It could vault you to financial success and independence— perhaps even wealth.

So get that nifty-looking notebook, make like a safari guide, and start tracking! In the next chapter we'll put that information to good use.

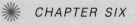 *CHAPTER SIX*

Chemo for Debt II:
A Plan That Pays

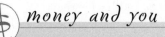 *money and you*

Take a moment to consider:

- Does your debt cause you to worry and experience stress?
- Have you clarified what is essential and nonessential spending for you?
- Do you spend to boost your self-esteem? If so, is it working?
- Is your choice to go into debt indicative that you believe you need more than God has given you?
- Do you feel powerless over your ability to control or put an end to your indebtedness?
- Do you ask first God to provide you with what you need, or do you simply use your best judgment, go ahead, and borrow and buy?

CREDIT IS MARKETED AGGRESSIVELY IN OUR CAPITAL-loving culture. Don't feel badly if you've succumbed—it's perfectly normal in our society. But don't feel you have to live with enormous debt to fulfill the American Dream. Just because credit, and therefore debt, is easy to acquire doesn't mean we should access it. (So are drugs. Easy doesn't mean it's right.) Though debtors' prisons no longer exist, we can still suffer in mental prisons of our own making. Take heed of Ogden Nash, who said, "Some debts are fun when you are acquiring them, but none are fun when you set about retiring them."

By doing the exercises in the previous chapter, you've learned about good and bad debt, and just where your money is going each day, week, and month. The next step is to use that information to formulate your two-pronged plan: one for paying off debt and the other for avoiding it in the future.

From this chapter, you should glean a few ideas for putting debt in its place. I encourage you to choose one—yes, just one—thing you can do to take a step in the direction of regaining control over your expenditures in order to curb and dissolve your debt.

That's right. This isn't a complex nineteen-step program to conquering the debt monster. It's a matter of finding one thing you can begin to do differently today. One change in your behavior can give you the hope and the energy to move out of the debt maze into financial victory.

Consider Anita. Year after year, she and her husband found themselves deeper in debt. Living in Southern California, the property value of their house soared, so each year, they refinanced, taking out equity, using it to pay down their bulging debt. She said, "We began to think of our house as a third income-producing adult in the family!"

Yet Anita knew things were only getting worse. She said, "It seemed I paid for that new picture in the living room three times over in agony, besides the interest I was paying on it." Anita and Keith went to a debt reduction seminar for help. The first thing they did was to consolidate their debt into one lower payment. They had been playing the credit card jumping game for a while but had gotten burned a few times by not reading the fine print about when rates would change or the minimum payment due.

Anita explains their slow recovery: "When first I dieted, I read all about food and realized I ate all the wrong things. I remember thinking if I would just make little changes in what I thought about eating, over time, I'd have no weight problem. I'd replace sodas with water, French fries with veggies, make it a habit, and no yo-yo waistline. The thing is, it's a little daily discipline, versus three months of killing yourself at the gym and starving yourself.

"The money issue is newer for me than the diet issue, but I decided money would work the same way. Engage in little daily disciplines, like turning the lights out, or not ordering out for pizza. My advice," says Anita, "is to find a little thing that you start to do differently every day. I formed good spending habits by simple repetition, which made it much easier to extricate myself from the rut of overspending."

Anita is now two years away from being debt-free (other than the mortgage, from which they're no longer siphoning equity every year). She says, "You have to take baby steps, because a big leap just doesn't do it, but it's worth it. Each month we experience the beauty of watching those numbers drop lower."

A Payoff Plan

Have your credit cards taken on a life of their own, enrolling in grad school to become professional acquisitionists? Make like a man, declare war, and take back your country! Start with existing debt and determine the highest dollar amount you can reasonably commit to paying on those balances each month. That's income minus fixed expenses and living needs. Decide for yourself what "needs" includes. The goal isn't punishment or austerity. Do you need a weekly manicure and monthly haircut and coloring? Maybe so. At least ask the question.

Squeeze out as much additional cash as you comfortably can for your monthly payments, even if it's only ten or fifteen dollars.

> We spend money we don't have to buy things we don't need to impress people we don't like.
>
> ✳ *M. Scott Peck* ✳

Allot your money as follows: Pay off the account with the smallest balance first, while you continue to pay minimum balances due on the other accounts. Even if its interest rate is not the highest, the victory you'll feel from polishing off one account will be a great motivator propelling you forward, much like the first pounds that drop off rapidly at the beginning of a diet. (So it's mostly water weight, but it's still an accomplishment, and it gives you a great psychological boost toward cutting into the fat.)

Next, put as much money as you can into paying off the account with the highest interest rate. Continue paying off accounts from highest to lowest rate. If you can, transfer balances from accounts with the higher interest rates to accounts with lower rates.

Contact creditors and negotiate lower rates. Explain that you have established a plan to pay off your accounts, and request reduced rates or temporary reductions in payments. Some creditors might do it. You won't know if you don't ask. Keep them informed. (If you are hesitant to call those creditors, there's a section later about credit counseling agencies that will help you.)

Calculate the approximate date you will have paid off all the debt. Plan a celebration (for which you pay cash, of course), or celebrate along the way. If you're like me, you'll create a little calendar to tack in your closet and cross off each month as it passes. Create a bar chart indicating the volume of debt you've paid to date. Or perhaps you'll establish little nonmonetary rewards as you go, such as spending an entire afternoon reading instead of housecleaning, or celebrating with a family dinner in the backyard with folding table, chairs, candles, and linens, or taking a two-hour lavender bath, or baking your favorite dessert (oops—food as reward, but just this once).

Let's look at Minerva's situation. She has decided that she can come up with an additional $50 per month to pay toward her credit card debt. By doing this, she will be debt-free in just under 2½ years.

		Minerva's Pay-off Plan		
Creditor	Beginning Balance	Minimum Payment Due	Interest Rate	Time to Pay-off Date
Sears	$502.43	$ 20.00	12.40%	2 years, 5 months
MasterCard	877.86	17.00	14.65	2 years, 5 months
Shell	131.03	10.00	19.74	3 months
Visa	1,490.49	31.00	15.40	1 year, 9 months

Minverva chooses to apply the $50 toward her Shell account, because it has the highest interest rate as well as the lowest balance. She's pumped when in only three months' time the account is paid in full. Next, she puts the $50 plus the $10 she had been paying on her Shell account toward her Visa debt, (along with the $31 minimum payment she had continued to make on Visa), now paying a total of $91 toward her Visa balance. Meanwhile, she continues to pay the minimum balance due on the other cards. When Visa is paid in full, she puts the $91 plus $17 toward her MasterCard account, until she is debt-free. Minerva has paid a total of $693.73 in credit card interest.

Had Minerva not made the additional payment of $50 per month toward her debt, she would have paid a total of $2,097.66 in interest and been debt-free in eight years.

When Willpower Isn't Enough

If the situation is looking volatile, call for backup. Contact an agency accredited by the National Foundation for Credit Counseling. Agencies often offer twenty-four-hour toll-free hotlines, free public education, and no initial fees. Search nfcc.org for an agency near you, or call their hotline at 800-388-2227. Counselors will review your debt and income and can create a feasible payoff plan in which you might make one monthly payment to the agency. The agency then forwards money to your creditors. A typical payment program takes three to four years. Where else were you planning to be in four years? You might as well be debt-free.

For this relatively painless service, you will be charged very little or nothing in fees because agencies often earn a percentage from the creditor for facilitating the payment, ensuring that the account remains current and the debt will be paid.

Creditors prefer such an arrangement for you to voluntarily repay, even with negotiated lower interest rates. It is a good deal for them, because collection agencies would charge significantly higher fees to recover your payments.

One such national agency is Springboard Non-Profit Consumer Credit Management (credit.org), which offers credit counseling, education, and a debt-management program. To arrange for a free and confidential counseling session by phone, call their twenty-four-hour hotline at 888-462-2227. If you are struggling to make minimum monthly payments, Springboard (and other agencies) can help by negotiating with your creditors to reduce interest charges and waive late and over-limit fees. The maximum fee Springboard will charge if you choose to use their debt-management program is twenty dollars a month.

If you are reticent to talk about all this to a human being right away, get some cyber-counseling. Log on to NFCC on-line counseling at nfcc.org.

Warning: Smoke out and avoid credit repair services that are costly scams or don't truly assist you. Do your homework and investigate the reputation and fine print of any service you're considering. Ask for a referral from friends.

You'll find great support at Debtors Anonymous meetings. These offer excellent opportunities to be encouraged and get motivated. Debtors Anonymous can be reached at 781-453-2743 or debtorsanonymous.org.

DA is based on the same principles as AA. I have attended a few meetings and found that the support offered is powerfully motivating to trim my spending even when I'm without financial troubles. Just hearing the debt difficulties the guy next to you is suffering lets you know you are not alone. You'll be grateful for the anonymity and nonjudgmental support you'll receive.

A Spending Strategy

Is there such a thing as a foolproof spending plan? Can you really avoid debt and be prepared, through wise financial planning, for every possible disaster? I won't deny that a series of unexpected economic hits can be financially devastating, even for people who are prudent with their money. An illness, investment loss, or job loss, compounded by unanticipated loss of medical or disability insurance, can be traumatic. This happened to several women in the homeless shelter where I volunteered.

But when I talk about creating a spending strategy, I'm talking about the things you *can* control, not the things you can't. You can do your best to maintain good physical health. (You can fasten your seat belt, look before you cross, and strap on that safety helmet.) You can do some things to combat disease. (You can exercise, floss, and spurn nicotine.) You can check to ensure that your insurance (medical, disability, auto, homeowner, renter) policies do not lapse. You can take steps to perform well on the job or begin to look for another if it appears yours is in jeopardy. You can set aside additional cash to be better prepared for the unexpected.

So you can't ensure against every possibility of financial loss. But you can do the grown-up thing: Accept responsibility for where you have gone wrong with your money. You can and must accept responsibility for what you can do differently and start anew.

> Failure can happen to anyone. It is what happens afterward that often matters most.
>
> ∗ Janice Maloney ∗

Honest, it can be done, and you're just the girl to do it! I know about miracles, because I've seen a few in my life. If you don't, then you're due for your share. The fact that this very moment you're reading this book versus the latest chick lit girl-from-London-shops-her-way-across-the-border is a good sign already! We've all fallen off the wagon once or a hundred times, and if you do, be quick to forgive yourself. Jesus said to forgive seventy times seven. I can't even think that high. The point is to keep on forgiving yourself. (If God will forgive you for your debt disasters, shouldn't you forgive yourself too?) If you ring up one of us (your support team), we'll lean over and hoist you right back up. Yes, it's hard, but so was algebra and so was aerobics. Simply pick yourself up, brush yourself off, and start over. Respect yourself. Respect your ability to get that spending plan in order.

Pay Cash for All New Purchases

This is a critical and first tactic. Do not add to those card balances, with the exception of a dire emergency. I use my credit card regularly and always pay the balance in full each month. But just for the exercise, and to ensure I don't suggest that you do something I've never tried myself, I committed to paying cash for a month. I'll admit, it was *not* easy. I suffered a battle with my inner impatient self to get in line to pay for gas. Sliding my card through the reader would have been so much easier and faster. You will, however, get comfortable with this over time, and I can't stress enough the importance of this tactic. Research indicates that when people pay with cash, they actually spend less than when using their credit cards.

Not using your credit card means *planning ahead*. We must actively plan to ensure we have enough cash on hand before heading to the grocery or hardware store.

Note: Do not allow your club dues, mobile phone bills, and Internet service provider bills to be charged to a credit card account unless you pay the credit card account in full each month. If you don't pay the card balance each month, you are effactually paying a premium for these services.

Close Credit Card Accounts

Once they're paid off, write to the card issuers, requesting that they close the accounts. Ask for a written confirmation documenting the closures. Then cut those cards into tiny pieces and toss.

Someone came up with the idea of placing your credit cards in water in the freezer so you will be forced to thoughtfully ponder your purchase while waiting for the ice to melt. Try that, but one problem is, you only need the number and expiration date to click and shop, or to call up Pottery Barn for delivery of a living room full of furniture.

To remove the temptation of a fresh new card, you can opt out of receiving preapproved offers of credit or insurance by calling 888-567-8688.

Run a Check on Yourself

What have those creditors been saying behind your back? Get a credit report and check it for accuracy. Make sure your closed accounts have, in fact, been properly closed. It's good to make sure your credit report is clean because errors take time to correct, and when you want to get the mortgage for the new house or refinance your old one, you can't wait months for those corrections to happen.

To request a copy of your current credit report, contact Equifax at 800-685-1111 (Equifax.com), Experian (Experian.com), or Trans Union at 800-888-4213 (transunion.com/index.jsp). Check to see if you meet criteria making you eligible to receive a free report. Otherwise, fees are typically nine dollars.

Save Those Receipts

Track all expenditures so you'll know exactly where you're coming from, where you are, and where you're going. For years I have kept an index card in my wallet with a running total of the current charges and balance on my charge account. When I sign a credit slip, I simply jot the name and amount of my purchase. When the account statement arrives, it takes me about ninety seconds to review it. I transfer anything that hasn't hit my account yet to a fresh index card. This tracking method is cheap, efficient, and works well for me. You may choose to use your hand-held computer. (Just last month I discovered a seventy-five-dollar error, which I would not have noticed without the quickie check.)

Raise Your Awareness

Examine every expense with the thought of eliminating fat. Exchange expenditures for nondollar replacements, such as bartering, creating from scratch (at least occasionally), enjoying fun

free stuff, or doing it for yourself. Why is it that often when wonderful things are free we simply value them less?

This buying test works well for me: When I discover an item I
hadn't planned to buy, I often wait two or three days, then head
back to the store. If it's still available, if I still want it, and I believe
it's a good value, then I figure it's meant to be. If it's gone, no
sweat—there are always, always, always more things to buy. Of
course, when I was on vacation in Bangkok and it was my last day,
that technique didn't work. I saw a gold bracelet I loved. So I bar-
gained, thought about it over lunch, and two hours later headed
back, pretty-colored currency in hand, and brought my bracelet
on home.

Trust me, I've made my share of impulsive, stupid, regrettable
purchases. There was the full fare I paid for a suit at Saks that
never did fit quite right except for a moment there when my
weight had achieved new heights of glory. I thought it made me
look slimmer. Rather, it thinned my wallet.

Get More Value from Every Dollar You Spend

This means don't fritter money on trinkets you'll display at next
year's garage sale, those tchotchkes from the seaside gift shop.
Hey, if you really enjoy collecting snow globes of the Eiffel
Tower, St. Louis Arch, and Golden Gate Bridge, then go crazy.
Nothing wrong with that. Just don't buy stuff you won't truly
value. Think before you buy. Put on mental armor before you
head to the mall.

If you find yourself taking carloads to the Salvation Army or
holding a garage sale every few years to empty out the shelves and
closets you continue to refill, that is a strong indicator you are buying too much unnecessary stuff.

Avoid Fiscal Obesity

Sacrifice breeds empowerment. Gluttony breeds impotence. Cutting back the first little bit will boost your self-esteem and help you feel you've gained control. Break that downward spiral of fading self-control by consciously forgoing one little-bitty thing. This small bit of abstinence will generate hope and lead to bigger victories.

See the Money around You

Consider any atypical source of cash as an opportunity to make a one-time chunk payment on your outstanding balances: tax refund, employment bonus, garage sale proceeds, freelance work, babysitting money. Cautiously consider selling some stock or other investments to wipe out the red, or cash in the Precious Moments collection that you inherited from Aunt Lottie on eBay.

Think of it this way: Any assets you have that you don't particularly need or want that might be sold for some coins, cost you real money just to sit on the shelf. The cost is the interest fees you are paying on any equivalent sum that remains in your credit card balance.

There is no way I'm suggesting you hock the family heirlooms. Just get conscious about managing your assets. Know where they are, and how much they're costing you.

Watch Less Television

In *The Overspent American,* Juliet B. Schor writes, "My research shows that the more TV a person watches, the more he or she spends. . . . What we see on TV inflates our sense of what's normal. The lifestyles depicted on television are far different from the average American's: With a few exceptions, TV characters are upper-middle-class, or even rich."[26]

Television undeniably inflates living standards. The *Friends* had low-paying jobs but flourished in New York apartments that an investment banker could barely afford. Then there is the endless stream of advertisements for things that promise to make you skinnier, blonder, smarter, more popular, or more beautiful, with the underlying assumption these are values to be sought.

Watching that constant parade of beautiful, fun things to buy directly correlates with excessive indebtedness. Professor of advertising James B. Twitchell concurs, "Television is the primary force in the material world."[27]

Think Positive

For a spending strategy to work, get your attitude straight. Adopt the half-full mentality, versus the half-empty one. A spending plan focuses on the money available to spend, unlike a budget, which focuses on constraint. Maintaining an attitude of deprivation will weaken your likelihood of success. Speak, think, believe—and even drink, walk, and sashay with an attitude of abundance. Then watch your life unfold.

And the Tortoise—She *Scores!*

You don't need the willpower of Arnold Schwarzenegger heading to the gym. A written plan and a sassy spirit will take you miles toward the finish line. Even if you slip down a wrong path and have to spend days backtracking to the main trail, you're still making progress because you're moving and you're correcting your (increasingly rare) errant turns! Your patience will be tested, because it takes turtlelike movements, not jackrabbit hops, to win the race. As I've heard it said, the race goes not to the swift, but to those who keep on running.

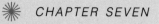

CHAPTER SEVEN

If Men Are from Home Depot, Women Are from Macy's

money and you

Take a moment to consider:

- What is the most recent thing someone influenced you to buy that you later regretted and perhaps never used, wore, or consumed?
- When have you felt guilt when buying something? Were those feelings valid or invalid?
- Do you typically shop when you're bored, lonely, angry, frustrated, or when you actually need something?
- When you shop, do you have to buy something before you go home?
- Have you ever engaged in a retail fast (abstinence)? How would it feel to even consider doing so for one month?
- Do you have any idea how much money you have spent on clothes, shoes, or jewelry in the last year?
- Do you find yourself with the compelling need to drink, drive, or wear status initials, i.e., Dom P, BMW, or DKNY?

FOR SOME PEOPLE, STRIDING INTO BLOOMINGDALE'S is like taking a hit of caffeine. First you rush through congested traffic to get a parking space close to the door. Tension is high as you grab your handbag, head for the brightly lit shop doors, and plunge inside. It's like piloting your F-14 Tomcat in for an abrupt landing on an aircraft carrier—you see the lights and glittery displays circling round as you gasp with shortened breath and take it all in. Adrenaline is taking its course.

Good thing you landed on that aircraft carrier because, girl-friend, it is a battle. Do you think retail stores exist as an act of societal beneficence? Trust me on this—their interests are quite at odds with yours. You need to get hip to what's going down. They've spent millions just to get you in the door. Yes, you (well, your dollars, anyway) are that special! They continue the seduction with fineries and trinkets that will be so *yesterday* within weeks and months, compelling you to come back for more.

Meanwhile, retailers and consumer-product companies are spending millions on retail consultants—analysts who excruciatingly analyze Jane Shopper's every move. Ought you not, at minimum, work up a countercampaign when you're out on the front lines? You pretty much have no choice but to be pressed back, your territory overtaken, if you're not armed with the intelligence needed to stand against the enemy. It's a David-and-Goliath battle, but as you recall, the little guy can win.

> Lead me not into temptation: I can find the way myself.
>
> * Rita Mae Brown *

If retailers are spending millions to figure out how to get into your pocketbook, then, honey, it's worth your time and effort to devise a few tactics to keep them out.

Simplicity Didn't Follow Me to the City

How much stuff do you think you use? Probably more than you could imagine. My friends consider me a low-maintenance gal. I don't wear a lot of makeup or get manicures. But I am a walking brand conglomerate. Before I leave my house in the morning, I've typically availed myself of Colgate, Glide, Listerine, Oil of Olay, TRESemmé, Bath & Body Works, Matrix Essentials, Lady Schick, Almay, Estée Lauder, Clinique, Lancôme, and Chanel. And I don't even wear perfume.

I've awakened to my Sony clock radio, turned off the Vicks room humidifier, used my Kohler shower, Helen of Troy hairdryer, Sony CD player, Kleenex, Q-tips, and of course, Northern Tissue.

Not a century ago, Grandma Durling washed up with Ivory soap in the morning and slipped her breakfast milk from the icebox, for which Grandpa Durling had chopped and stored ice from the lake. (The cows on the back forty had been milked the evening before.) Then Grandma was good to go. At this rate, what will it take my grandchildren to get ready for their day?

How much of what we believe we need only recently *did not exist?*

Retail anthropologist Paco Underhill wrote, "Clearly, possession is an emotional and spiritual process, not a technical one."[28] So it's out. The secret retailers didn't want you to know: They flagrantly pursue—*not* the satiation of your emotional and spiritual cravings, but the stoking of your urges so that, annuity-like, you'll come back for more, continuously leaving your dollars in their coffers.

The *New York Times* recounted a father's trip to the grocery with his children Theo, four and a half; and Virginia, two and a half.

> I took the kids to the supermarket, and in aisle 1, each kid stopped to grab something, with Pokémon, Harry Potter, Winnie the Pooh, or some other attractive nuisance on it. By aisle 3, it was getting to be too much and I said, "Look, these boxes have nothing to do with Winnie the Pooh or Harry Potter. They don't eat the food or use the toothpaste. The people who make this stuff simply put it on the box so that you will want to buy it."
>
> The kids were a bit subdued for a few aisles. In aisle 10, Theo looked up at me and at the boxes there and said, "It's working. It's working."[29]

I was admiring the cashmere and wool blend coat my date was wearing last night. He responded, "Bought it at Costco. Every time I go there, I can't get out of the store without spending at least two hundred dollars. I see all this stuff I never knew I needed."

Why not respect yourself more than all the places you spend your money? Why not pay yourself instead of the ad agencies, boutique owners, and e-tailers that are eternally eager to cash in on *your* future financial security and retirement? Put your money into your savings and investments, not a trip to the neighborhood boutique. The beautiful truth is: *We are free to choose what we do with every cent we have.*

All Roads Lead to the Mall

It all started when Eve took a nibble on that apple and then realized she had absolutely nothing to wear. Next thing you know, it was coordinates for spring, summer, and fall; business casual, at-home, and formal; sportswear, cruise wear, and beachwear.

We would do well to take note of the problem of Eve. When she succumbed to the temptation of the apple, forgoing all the mangoes, kiwi, and plums a girl could eat, it simply opened the door to more desires, propelling her, handbag-first, into the vast land of dissatisfaction. Bumped out of the Garden of Eden, she became the first woman to suffer abandonment issues, creating an entire new field of study for psychiatrists to probe.

> We heap up around us things that we do not need as the crow makes piles of glittering pebbles.
>
> ✳ *Laura Ingalls Wilder* ✳

Is it possible to resist the apple in your life, lest it serve to destroy your hope for life in the garden? What's your apple? (Mine is shoes, but that's another story.)

Birds do it; bees do it. Shopping. Like eating, sleeping, and breathing, it's the activity common across all species. Watch birds, beavers, even piglets in action if you don't believe it. They're all shopping—for food, for housing supplies, for a mate. Wolves can travel thirty miles in one day scouring the countryside for food, without tiring.[30] I've known a few chickadees who can shop those formidable outlet malls with equal determination. Shopping is an innate human propensity—but an urge stronger for some than others.

In the twentieth century, shopping became a reprieve for homebound housewives. It evolved into a social event as malls built community spaces and teens swarmed the food courts. Soon, seniors arrived in droves attired in colorful jogging suits for morning power walks followed by midday power shopping for knickknacks to collect dust on the console TV.

In our culture, shopping is the end. Consumption is not a conduit, a pathway elsewhere—it's the main event. It's not just about the stuff bought. Sometimes when we shop, it doesn't matter *what* we've purchased, just that we've bought something—anything—or else it will have been an unfruitful trip, an unsuccessful chase. What disappointment it is to return empty-handed from a day's hunt, no prize game in hand.

> We are kept out of the Garden by our own fear and desire in relation to what we think to be the goods of our life.[31]
>
> ✳ *Joseph Campbell* ✳

Why We Shop

Shopping as Escape

Enid Levinger's pattern is to head directly to the stores after a doctor's appointment. She thinks, *Whew! I'm OK, now I can shop.* She doesn't know whether it's out of relief . . . or a reward for surviving.

Jeanie says she shops to dissipate anger. Her neighbor Maribeth shops for respite after caring for three young children at home all day. These two cul-de-sac queens are on the right track. They are highly self-aware and did not hesitate when I asked them what was the emotional basis for their shopping.

Sometimes we shop because it makes us feel better, taller, thinner, happier, prettier, more sophisticated, more red-headed, more athletic, and more intelligent. We shop because we need a pick-me-up, we got a promotion, we didn't get a promotion, we broke up with our boyfriend, we got a new boyfriend, we're on vacation, we deserve a vacation, because we earned it, and because we deserve a special treat for how hard we've studied, slaved, saved, sweltered, and sacrificed.

Shopping both relieves and creates tension. It relieves frustration, anxiety, boredom, anger, and sadness. It helps us organize and fraternize; it makes us sweeter, kinder, and more thoughtful. Shopping excites, making the forager feel powerful and sexy. Shopping is used as psychotherapy, bribery, to get even with our spouse, to distract our children, or as a reward for simply surviving another bad day.

Shopping as Entertainment

Shopping has evolved into an interactive experience. Its entertainment value is often bigger than the things you're purchasing. Stores are destinations. Restaurants are more about the experience, less about the food: Rainforest Café—"a wild place to shop and eat"; Tommy Bahama—"a day for looking good and feeling even better"; and Hard Rock Café—"party like a rock star."

I spend hours in Barnes & Noble, invited by the overstuffed furniture and coffee bar. The Chicago Nike store seemed much like a fun house last time I was there to restock my sock supply. The American Girl Place is like a store with training wheels, intended to arouse the shopping hormone in prepubescent girls. This hyperstimulating experience includes fine dining and live theater. Travelers from around the globe wait behind red velvet ropes to cram into the store during the Christian high holidays.

Shopping as Religion

For the highly evolved consumer, shopping has become both art and science. To what degree has your shopping experience advanced—beginner, graduate, or Ph.D.? In *Confessions of a Shopaholic*, shopping was a sensual experience for the fictional character Rebecca Bloomwood. She muses:

> I count out the money in tens and twenties and wait, almost shivering as [the clerk] ducks behind the counter and produces the green box. She slides it into a thick glossy bag with dark green cord handles and hands it to me, and I almost want to cry out loud, the moment is so wonderful. . . . That moment. That instant when your fingers curl round the handles of a shiny, uncreased bag—and all the gorgeous new things inside it become yours. What's it like? It's like going hungry for days, then cramming your mouth full of warm buttered toast. It's like waking up and realizing it's the weekend. It's like the better moments of sex. Everything else is blocked out of your mind. It's pure, selfish pleasure.[32]

For Rebecca, the experience becomes religious. Upon arriving home, she opens the box and reverentially lifts the scarf from the folded tissue. She says, "For a moment we are both silent. It's as though we're communing with a higher being. The god of shopping."[33] Even the book title is suggestive of sin and the booth where Catholics go to acknowledge their wrongs.

Dumb Things I Have Done in High-End Department Stores

Lest you think I'm above shopping craziness, let me relate a true tale. The stupidest purchase I ever made was when I was limited for time, feeling fat, and had a blind date with a guy whose photo looked so much like Tom Cruise. I spent way too much money on an outfit that slimmed my backside about an inch but didn't look particularly great overall. (I only noticed this a week later.) I wore the outfit so infrequently that the CPW (cost per wearing) was exorbitantly high.

I actually repeated this shopping mistake. (Note to self: Never go shopping for outfit that I absolutely need in twenty-four hours to make me look ten pounds thinner on first date. If must buy something, settle for new lipstick, then head home to soak in bath and figure out clever hairstyle.)

Only twice in my life have I bought an outfit for a specific date. So fitting it was that both dates had to be canceled! One was with an ex-boyfriend, and it's probably a jolly good thing we never reconnected. The second was for the Cruise look-alike, who, after he saw my photograph, apparently decided I wasn't Gwyneth Paltrow enough. Another save!

So I had two beautiful overpriced outfits, one so tight I couldn't breathe while sitting; the other looked sloppy as it grazed my curves. This is what happens when you buy in a panic, or with way too much thought for your hips.

The fact is, shopping for the wrong reasons has enormous downsides. When we focus on our own needs, wants, and desires, we become ingrown and selfish—I believe a part of us actually starts to atrophy or rot. We can no longer see others' needs because we are mesmerized by the things we aspire to acquire. We lose awareness, becoming desensitized to the needs of the hungry, poor, lonely, and homeless—the neighbor who needs bus fare and grocery money. We become conscientious objectors in the war on poverty and do not recognize our resources as the opportunity they present.[34] We cannot comprehend others' needs when we are looking at ourselves. For many of these same reasons, alcoholics turn to their numbing devices. Others raid the fridge. Still others don outfits four sizes too small and head out on the town looking for attention and getting it, but not the kind that makes their hearts swell with true joy.

I long ago discovered that when I am at my most emotionally desperate place is when I have the greatest need to reach out and give to others, experiencing empathy with their needs. That heals. Shopping doesn't.

A Reconnaissance Mission

Get your little soul ready *before* you find yourself in a position where you are mooning over something you must strain so hard not to buy. Mentally put yourself in the place of how you will feel when you see something you simply must have, or when you spend the weekend at your friend's gorgeous vacation home after you've just downsized yourself to a cramped apartment. Plan ahead. Brace yourself. Take action to manage your feelings. While it's better to own them than stave them off, it's certainly right to act contrarily to those emotions' whiny, selfish demands.

What this means is, put the situation into perspective. Painful as it will be, dig for the root cause of your feelings of inferiority, sadness, frustration, self-pity, or fatigue. (I mean, is it *really* about the new leather jacket that everyone owns but you? The trip to Antigua, Bali, or Chattanooga that "everyone" is taking this winter? Is it *truly* about the scaled-down party for your kid you're throwing at home, while your colleague is taking her child's ten best friends to an amusement park for a weekend of birthdaying?) Perspective helps. You're not in bed with your neighbor or colleague. You do not know how she feels when she closes her eyes at night. You do not know if she's even *sleeping* at night—without medication. You don't know what fears pound at her mental footing, what prognosis she got from her child's psychiatrist or how long it's been since her husband touched her. There is so much you don't know; the tiny sliver you do know is simply not valid for her entire experience. So don't go feeling sorry for your lone self because you cannot see the complete picture.

The Reason You Live—Er, Shop

So, back to you. Do you shop in italics? Is shopping a problem for you? I mean, enjoying it is perfectly fine. (I find it fatiguing, so more power to you if it's fun and energizing for you.) But do you find yourself at home with stuff you didn't intend to buy and, in fact, regret? You know, those morning-after receipts and tags and bags. Perhaps you rush to put the things away so your husband won't notice all you've bought. Take this quiz to check whether you buy things for purposes other than meeting reasonable needs. (Only you can determine "reasonable," because you know your means and resources; I don't.)

Shopping and Feeling

Check True or False

( ) T ( ) F   1. I feel an emotional high when returning from a shopping excursion.

( ) T ( ) F   2. I frequently regret making purchases.

( ) T ( ) F   3. I often intend to return items but end up keeping them whether I use them or not.

( ) T ( ) F   4. I rationalize my way out of shopping guilt.

( ) T ( ) F   5. I'm not happy if I can't shop every week. (Groceries don't count.)

( ) T ( ) F   6. I often rush out to buy what my girlfriends picked up on sale.

( ) T ( ) F   7. My mantra: Outlet malls—God's gift to womankind.

( ) T ( ) F   8. I often turn to shopping after having a fight with someone, suffering a loss, or experiencing a depressing day.

( ) T ( ) F   9. I get agitated if I haven't been to the mall in several weeks.

( ) T ( ) F 10. I'm uncomfortable at a party if I'm not wearing a new outfit and accessories.

Taming the Shopping Shrew

Good news: You don't have to be a slave to your shopping whims. Here are some startlingly easy-to-apply ideas for bringing the shopping shrew into captivity—and shopping smarter when you do hit the sidewalks.

Analyze before You Buy

Answer these key questions. They could save you bundles. When you've a decision to make—big or small—flush it out not by asking, "Can I afford it?" but better these defining questions:

- Is this expenditure congruent with my values and the purpose of my life?
- Will I receive fulfillment and value in proportion to the energy I expended to earn this money?

Do Not Spend on a Whim

OK, maybe a stick of gum. Most assuredly, never buy a big-ticket item extemporaneously. You'd not believe the people who buy a new car, boat, or vacation home largely to scratch a sudden impulsive itch.

One guy drove into a car dealership to claim a prize (a cheap transistor radio shaped like a sports car) and came out with new car and matching payments for the next five years. His wife, who worked two jobs while he was in graduate school, was not pleased. Just the day before, the two had agreed to postpone replacing the worn sofa because of their meager finances.

Dorothy, a single woman in her late thirties, was living paycheck to paycheck when she saw a television ad for a new car for an amazingly low $149 per month. It seemed too good to be true, and indeed, it was. She didn't need a new car, but drove off the lot later that afternoon, having been sweetly but savagely seduced into payments of $279 per month. That car was repossessed within the year (but the salesguy happily pocketed his commission).

That Package Isn't Cheap

Often the ingredients in the four-dollar drugstore cosmetics are nearly the same as in the forty-dollar department store brand that comes with elegant wrappings and a free cheap plastic carryall. Same goes for some luxury cars.

Don't Shop When Tired, Sad, Frustrated

Avoid situations in which you would be tempted to compromise your money values, such as stopping at the mall en route home after a long day of travel, squabbles, and disappointment, or logging onto your favorite e-tailers once you collapse at home.

> When women are depressed they either eat or go shopping. Men invade another country.
> ✳ Elayne Boosler ✳

While recovering from surgery, a broken heart, or the death of a loved one is simply not the time to make significant financial decisions or set out on a shopping spree. In fact, the single most valuable thing you can incorporate into such a process is time itself. Time gives perspective and helps you consider your real needs and motives for your choices.

Mail Check!

Don't open the gift catalogs proffering shiny, smooth, beautiful, lovely items. Better yet, call their toll-free numbers and request to be removed from the mailing list. I've winnowed my mail down to a minimum, for which my longtime letter carrier, Rodney—not to mention the forests—thanks me.[35] (See notes for information on having your name removed from advertisers' lists.)

Wait Three Days before Making a Purchase

Or a month before a major one. This gives you time to *get conscious* about your decisions: Do you really need it? Will you still want it tomorrow? If the item is still available—great! If it's not or the sale is over, it wasn't meant to be yours. Don't think about it; just get over it. There will always be more.

Research On-line

Compare prices at consumerreports.org, mysimon.com, and dealtime.com. Review quality, durability, usage, and other consumers' comments. I spent a few hours at the Consumer Reports site before confidently heading out to make one stop to buy a new car. A year later I've no regrets. Shop on-line for the best prices. Check priceline.com, travelocity.com, cheaptickets.com, ebay.com, or ubid.com.

Skip the Social Shopping

I get caught up urging my friends to go ahead and buy stuff I wouldn't spend my own money on. Socialize less often (in-store) with your friends who are big into shopping and acquiring.

Know Why You Buy

Recognize that much of what we buy is prestige, and prestige is expensive. Separate wants from necessities so you'll know which is which, and make appropriate decisions with that knowledge.

You'd Better Shop Around

I spent only twenty minutes to find the same stove at two stores, just two miles and fifty dollars apart. Comparison shopping can save a bundle. You'd be amazed how uncompetitive some merchants are. They count on lazy people like me not to notice their higher markups. I wouldn't recommend driving across town to save forty cents on a hair clip, however. I do have one friend whose greatest pleasure is driving across the entire Chicago area to save a few cents. I guess it's just her hobby.

Plan Ahead

Save up until it's not a financial pinch to buy. Anticipation is sometimes the best part. You'll appreciate it more. In my poorer days, I planned to buy one item a year. I'm serious: The first year I bought a bed; the second, a microwave oven; the third, a piano; and the fourth, a television. I didn't mind waiting because I didn't miss what I'd not yet had. (Life was good sans recycled sitcoms.)

Buy Used

Buy stuff with a little experience under its belt. I buy used books on-line, except for gifts—thus the differentiation between frugal (used books for me) and cheap (that would be used books for others). I shop at consignment stores in upscale neighborhoods. It's more fun to have almost-new stuff from Neiman Marcus at a wee percentage of its original cost that someone else gained too much weight to wear any longer. I'm no fashionista, so I don't mind wearing clothes a few months or even a season past their "sell by" date. I get the most compliments on my faux-fur trimmed jacket someone else bought at Neiman Marcus that I picked up for twenty-eight bucks. (I love it when other people spend money and I get the goods!) This goes for furniture too.

Pay Attention to Add-Ons

I bought a new stove, forgoing the upgraded model that, for an additional $150, offered a cooler-looking grill top that the salesguy hyped as *de rigueur*. I decided I'd not notice the difference and kept the $150. I didn't get the car battery charger for my mobile phone because I head out prepared, charging it at home.

Know the Real Cost

Think you can spot the cost of something by its price tag? Think again, oh noble shopper. That blouse may cost three times as much as you think if you charge it and pay interest on it longer than the length of time you keep the blouse. Then you've paid Social Security, Federal, state, local income taxes, and sales taxes. It costs you to get to work, pay childcare, set aside a percentage of earnings into retirement, savings, and charity. It costs to clean, insure, and maintain stuff you bought. A dollar saved (considering taxes and additional expense) is nearly two dollars earned. The price tag may read $59.99, but the actual cost is, say, $119.99. Are you OK with working hard to earn money in October to pay the principal and interest on an Italian dinner you digested in April? I'm just asking . . .

Track Your Spending

My shopper friends unanimously agree on my number one, most-effective, favorite, and user-friendly technique for maintaining a check on spending impulses. Its efficiency is in its simplicity and the cognizance it offers. As I mentioned earlier, I never make a credit card purchase without jotting the name of the store, service, or vendor next to the sum spent on a bright-colored three-by-five index card. My wallet is never without that index card tucked between the bills and my single credit card, and I always know just how much I've recently spent.

Today Is Day One

So what if you've been paying full retail, buying tons of stuff, and feel it's too late to change? That was yesterday and you're not like that anymore—starting today. I used to pay full retail on Michigan Avenue for my wardrobe. Then my girlfriend Amelia started taking me to discount stores. I needed good clothes for client meetings, so thought I should pay good prices too. Slowly, I began to put other expenditures in check as well.

I am not suggesting you ignore your desires completely. Just don't be average. Go ahead and embrace luxuries. (Jesus led a largely abstemious lifestyle, yet he allowed a woman to pour an entire half-liter of perfume costing a year's wages on his feet.[36]) Just don't get swept into stifling superficiality—or painful debt. Go ahead and vacation in France every summer. But you just might choose to fly business class instead of first, or coach instead of business. You might wear some little sandals from Old Navy or a previously owned designer dress with your silk Hermès scarf while strolling the Riveria. Mix it up, but shoot for spending below your means—the secret to living financially free.

CHAPTER EIGHT

The Road to Wealth: Save Early, Invest Regularly

money and you

Take a moment to consider:

- Have you calculated how much money you'll have and the age you'll be able to retire given your current savings and investment rates?
- Could you be subconsciously waiting for your prince to come (or inheritance or lottery windfall to drop) to take care of your financial needs?
- Do you know how much money you saved last month? Last year?
- Did you save *any* money last month or last year?
- Do you flip the channels or turn the page when financial market news comes on?
- Do you procrastinate investing because of ignorance, boredom, fear of loss, or another reason?
- Do you review your investment account statements within two days of their arrival?
- How do you respond to a sharp drop in the markets or stocks in which you're invested?
- Do you tend to take greater risks with your career, physical challenges, and personal relationships than with your money?

I HAVE NEVER GONE TO THE AIRPORT WITHOUT A destination in mind and a bit of luggage in tow. You wouldn't go to the international terminal without your passport or without having made arrangements for lodging and transportation at your final destination. The good thing about being a girl is we're usually prepared. We've got whatever we need in our purse (at least one woman in the group has everything from postage stamps to bug spray). We're good at organizing our social calendars, we don't mind following instructions, and we can read maps. We're generally able to make our way through life with just a little help from our friends and some clear road signage.

We are also willing to learn from history, especially from such charismatic leaders as Winston Churchill. On 28 November 1934, our man Churchill addressed Parliament, saying, "I do not believe that war is imminent, and I do not believe that war is inevitable. But it seems very difficult to resist the conclusion that if we do not begin forthwith to put ourselves in a position of security, it will soon be beyond our power to do so."[37]

You may not believe that financial failure is imminent, and you may not believe that financial ruin is inevitable. But it seems very difficult to resist the conclusion that if you do not begin forthwith to put yourself in a position of financial freedom, it will soon be beyond your power to do so. Noah didn't wait for the rain.

Girls Going to (Stock) Market

The financially savvy woman keeps things simple. She plans to spend, she plans to save, and she plans to invest. She knows what's coming in and what's going out, so when she sees the great deal on a car, coat, or cantaloupe, she has a good idea right away whether it will work with her financial plan. Once she tucks her dollars aside for savings, she does a little mental compartmentalization and never again thinks of them as spendable money. She also has an ear tuned to the capital markets—just enough to ensure she is following simple investment principles and sticking to basic investment strategies that will keep her in nail polish through the year 2057.

> In the house of the wise are stores of choice food and oil, but a foolish man devours all he has.[38]
>
> ✳ King Solomon ✳

How does she do this? Read on for simple strategies that will take you to well-planned financial freedom.

Spend Less Than You Earn (Act Your Wage)

She knows that as painful as it may be to start saving now (and it feels much less painful once she's in the groove of it), it will be far more painful later *not* to have saved. The final hurdle this savvy female crosses is investing. She forges ahead, unintimidated by marketspeak peppered with violent war and sports analogies and multisyllabic financial terms that media professionals and Wall Street wizards toss about to appear particularly erudite. (Yes, egos thrive on Wall Street just like power does inside the Beltway.)

May I take a moment to point out that the sisterhood of financially savvy women consists of high-school dropouts and Ph.D.s alike; neurologists, weight-loss counselors, and real-estate developers; fourth-generation African-Americans, Romanian immigrants, retirees, singles, marrieds, with child or not—you get the idea. That's the funny thing about investments—they don't know about racism, sexism, classism, or even IQ.

Let's make that to *our* advantage. If you're concerned that women still make around seventy-two cents on the dollar to men and live longer on smaller pensions, well, one thing's for sure: Money is the great equalizer. Investments are equal-opportunity. Chicks can make or lose just as much money as the guys!

What Miss Money Smart does figure out that Miss Financially Frivolous is going to learn (as soon as she reads this book) is that to enjoy financial freedom, she must start right off tending to her inner penniless self. Once she's mined the deep within to determine her true values and accompanying goals, she's good to go with a plan for the big three: spending, saving, investing. Because she's focused on why she acquires and how to uproot the reasons she buys stuff and services she doesn't truly want or need, it becomes far easier to pay herself first. She doesn't spend up until her accounts are empty; she sets money aside out of her earnings. Miss Money Smart knows that saved money is cool money, fun money, popular money. It always looks good on her bank statement and never goes out of style.

Save What You Haven't Spent
(Out of Sight, Out of Reach)

I'm serious about that "pay yourself first" stuff. If you decide to make a written spending plan, you'll want to include a column for "savings" in the "stuff I need" section (which includes items such as housing expense, utilities, and groceries). You'd do well to choose a fixed amount to deposit into savings with each paycheck. Even better is to arrange for automatic deposit from your paycheck or checking account, coinciding with your pay periods.

I do it the other way around. Most of my earning life, I have earned commissions so my paychecks were never the same from month to month. I lived on a sum quite below my average monthly earnings and deposited the overage into a money market fund every month. When you save money, do it purposefully—with a destination, a mission—or it won't be as meaningful, fun, or successful. Save with an eye on your goals.

Do I hear a few of you saying, "I can't afford to put money in a 401(k) or IRA account"? The fact is, honey, you can't afford not to. The sooner you start, the less pain, greater reward, higher satisfaction, and more financial freedom you will experience. Trust me. The trade-off is this: a little pain and discomfort now, or a huge amount of pain and discomfort in your old age.

The Early Bird Gets the
Shuffleboard Court

Many people don't plan for retirement, hoping they'll be well enough to work until the day they die. But we don't get to choose when and where death will find us. Those nonsavers who claim they don't save for retirement because they plan to work until they die would do well to tour a retirement center, nursing home, or hospital, or look at statistics for stroke and disability among the elderly.

There is a simple fundamental rule to saving for retirement: start early. Barring that, if you're in the afternoon nap of your life, wake up and start when you can—that is, now. Remember: We do what we *can* do, not what we *can't*. An early start will allow you to begin retirement, or a partial retirement, while your health is still good enough for you to hit the bicycle trail, golf course, or sailboat, as it were.

Are you postponing saving for retirement for the instant gratification of a double mocha latte? Did you return from the county fairgrounds with Elvis memorabilia you never knew you wanted? Did you know that $83 saved per month (that's $1,000 per year), earning a return of 10 percent (that's still lower than the previous seventy-five years' average return on stocks of 12 percent[39]), you will have $9,390 in five years, $24,500 in ten years, and a sweet $680,910 in forty years? Of course that's in today's dollars, before inflation, deflation, or no flation.

Saving Early Totally Rocks!

So you don't shuffle? Or you're not about to trade in your surfboard for a shuffleboard? No sweat. There are other advantages to starting your retirement fund before you've begun shopping for a wedding dress or baby carriage. Saving early has its advantages:

- You're more likely to retire while still in mountain-biking, twenty-foot-wave-surfing shape.
- You'll earn higher investment returns per savings output. You'll enjoy the time value of money because money saved

early works longer. This refers to the incredible power of compound interest, which has been said to be the eighth wonder of the world. It's like getting somebody else to work for *you!*

- It allows you more flexibility to move elsewhere or change careers. And don't assume you'll bulk up by saving big sums in your later years. Job markets are dicey; industries are changing faster than ever. Even doctors lose jobs. You may need to retool and take a lower salary. Don't assume your income is on a permanent upward trajectory. Another problem: You'll have to adjust to a less pricey lifestyle if you've been spending all your earnings. It's tough to sharply adjust your standard of living to begin saving in later years.

- It allows you to take much greater risks offering greater rewards. Because of the longer time horizon, you're more likely to make up losses you may incur with taking bigger investing risks.

- You don't worry so much when the stock market takes huge hits. You're in for the long haul. You're not sweating about having to select the next star performer to beat the market in an attempt to play catch-up.

Need I say it? If your company will match a portion of your contributions to retirement savings, *do it!* Don't leave one dime that could be yours lying on the ground, especially if it's a gift from your employer.

Invest What You've Saved

Once savings have begun to accumulate in a bank savings deposit account or money market fund, it's time to go investing.

It's funny that this step is so frequently overlooked or avoided.
We can get so overwhelmed with investment information, mul-
tiple options, and conflicting opinions, we don't know what to do
or how to invest and end up doing the easiest thing: nothing. Like
a deer in headlights, like a kid in a candy
store, like being accepted at all five col-
leges to which you applied, you're hit
with the stun gun of indecision. Not act-
ing on a choice *is* a decision, and probably
not the one you'd actually have chosen.

> Do something,
> even if it's wrong!
> * U.S. Treasury
> bond trader *

And it's not just option overload that stalls us at this point.
Because we're so afraid to take risks and make mistakes, we do
nothing at all. Better to work off a rough draft plan than to be
launched adrift in the choppy seas of a consumerist culture.

You've Got It Going On

Have no fear: If you passed fourth grade math and reading (which,
if you're reading this, I think you have), you're set with the fundamental technical skills essential to effectively manage your investments. Additional essential soft skills are discipline, patience, and
consistent behavior. Women, especially mothers, are generally well
practiced in these skills. Explaining or having the ability to pro-
nounce the Pythagorean theorem is not essential to investing
well. Nor should you be intimidated by marketspeak. The lingo
characteristic of traders and money managers is no different from
slang that evolves in other lines of work. If you can plan a vacation,
you can formulate a draft savings and investment plan, and that's a
great place to start.

Set aside a little cash, read a primer on mutual funds (get a current personal finance magazine or library book), or surf your way through a premier investing site such as morningstar.com just to stick your toe in the pool and test the temperature. Join the American Association of Individual Investors (aaii.com) for an annual membership fee of forty-nine dollars to receive practical information and how-to guides for personal financial planning. Membership includes a monthly journal, local chapter meetings, invitations to seminars in your area about analyzing and managing investments, and other resources.

> People spend more time figuring out what restaurant they want to go to than they do researching their manager, their stock, or their mutual fund.
>
> ∗ Marc Cohodes ∗

Financial writer Peter Di Teresa said, "It usually takes a long time for investors to become sophisticated enough to realize how simple investing can be."[40] In an article titled "The Myth of the Dumb Investor," Jonathan Clements wrote, "You're so incompetent that you need outside help, right? Don't believe it. Indeed, among the 180,000 members of the American Association of Individual Investors, only 12 percent currently use a financial planner."[41]

Investing is simply committing your money to an entity with the expectation of earning a financial return for having done so. You can put your money to work, twenty-four hours a day, reaping returns while you sleep! Cool!

Investing will require time, consideration, and the ability to make decisions and take risks without knowing precisely the results you'll achieve. (Because nobody knows everything that will happen tomorrow.) You may think you know what is likely to happen in the morning or next spring, and you may be right, but there is a reason they call those publications *news*papers—the stuff written in there was not known the day before.

Risk, Sweet Risk

Don't let perfectionism get in the way, causing you to avoid investing entirely. Risk is good for you. Acknowledge it, get to know and understand it, and respect it. Take it out for lunch; the familiarity will ease your incertitude. Women may be more risk averse than men in part because they are rightfully concerned about their ability to remain financially solvent. Women live longer, so their money must last longer. They have typically contributed to pension plans for a shorter period (with time out for childbearing and child rearing). Women also have less of that risk hormone—testosterone.

> Nothing will ever be attempted if all possible objections must be first overcome.
> ✳ *Samuel Johnson* ✳

I am so girl. I regret my early fear to accept higher financial risk. Because of that my investment portfolio got off to a slow start, setting me back during the all-important early years. But regret is a complete waste of energy, so I focus on the bold risks I *have* successfully taken—in my career, finances, relationships (*yes,* I did *so* go out with that guy), and physical challenges. I'm so pleased that I went mountain biking in Italy, over rocks and stuff, so fast the air felt like a wall against my face. It totally boosted my self-esteem. Doing scary stuff like that helps me accept greater risks in other areas of my life, and on and on.

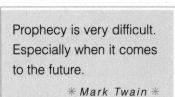

> Prophecy is very difficult. Especially when it comes to the future.
> ✳ *Mark Twain* ✳

May I remind you that simply being alive is a risk. Staying in bed is risky. I recall the story of a perfectly normal woman with no history of sleeping problems who awoke a quadriplegic, having injured her neck as she oddly vaulted over the footboard in her sleep. Getting married is a risk. A soaring divorce rate has not prevented the happily besotted from striding down the aisle—have you seen a shortage of brides lately? Me neither. Nuclear war has seemed imminent for decades. Jaywalking can maim. Aspartame has its dangers. Styrofoam cups have been cited as potentially carcinogenic.[42]

> Behold the turtle. He makes progress only when he sticks his neck out.
>
> ✳ James B. Conant ✳

Being alive is scary, when you think about it. You'd be much safer dead. Crawling out of bed in the morning and stepping into the shower can be as treacherous as rock climbing. Perfectly healthy folk have been known to slip and die of head trauma in their own double-headed, slate-lined steam shower.

Showering is risky. Not showering is riskier. Think bacteria buildup, odor, and social ostracism. Investing is risky. Not investing is riskier. Think loss of purchasing power, the poor farm, and social ostracism. Risk is our friend. It's what we want and undertake to make achievements and win rewards. It's not just about *peril*, but *opportunity*. Traders head to their markets each morning purposefully scouting for risks to undertake. Floor traders eat risk for breakfast. The motto goes: No risk—no reward. You can't win if you don't play. Successful investing incorporates conscious and measured exposure to risk without which you'd not have the opportunity for capital appreciation and income.

Risk is good. When you risk trying out for the basketball team, you might make it. When you put yourself out there for a hotly competitive job interview, you may get the offer. When Columbus set sail on the ocean blue, the odds were well against him, but he got a whole country (Colombia) and a holiday (Columbus Day) named for him. To honor such a gutsy guy, banks and financial markets close on his behalf for an entire day every October.

Without risk, life would have little meaning. Without risk, what would be the fun of snowboard-

> Everything is sweetened by risk.
>
> *Alexander Smith*

ing, dating, sales calls, new recipes, and birthing a baby? Take risks with your eyes, ears, and intuition wide open. Every financial decision you make incorporates weighing the risks and opportunities. Keeping all your savings in a bank savings account or bank CD is as dangerous but more foolish than that slippery rock climb. The greater risk you have undertaken is the lost opportunity of capital appreciation essential to keep pace with and exceed inflation. So you do retain the principal and gain interest earned, but meantime, you've lost purchasing power.

Don't let your money go stale in a bank savings account. Take it for a walk around the block, give it some air, and discover some new ways to put it to use. Sure, retaining three or six months' worth of living

> Avoiding danger is no safer in the long run than outright exposure; the fearful are caught as often as the bold.
>
> *Helen Keller*

expenses in a bank savings account is a totally appropriate risk exposure. The opportunity it provides is assurance of available cash, should the need arise.

We lose things. Keys, mittens, boyfriends, ten-dollar bills, business deals, and sometimes hope. Life is about loss and change. Nobody's monetary position is static, because the world isn't static. Portfolio values don't always trend steadily upward, although they have been known to do so—sometimes for years. Some investments hit hugely disorienting turbulence and collapse, never quite able to return to their former glorious heights. Don't let those few sway your nerve. Get in the game. It's completely normal to be concerned about the stability of your money, especially when stock prices lately have made mercury look stable. Don't sweat it; fear is good. It keeps you alive and on the edge of your seat. Would you prefer a financial life equivalent to huddling in the corner of your brown velour La-Z-Boy?

Your Risk Tolerance

Check out your fear factor. Take the following quiz to get a look at your risk profile.

( ) T ( ) F   1. I would have no problem going out on a blind date (if I were unmarried).

( ) T ( ) F   2. I would enjoy a job in which my income was irregular, such as based on commissions generated.

( ) T ( ) F   3. I have changed my hair color or hairstyle in the last year.

( ) T ( ) F   4. I enjoy legal gambling at casinos and race-tracks or by buying lottery tickets.

( ) T ( ) F   5. I enjoy engaging in dangerous sports such as skydiving, skiing, scuba diving, or mountain biking.

( )T ( )F   6. I would consider trying a new recipe when hav-
             ing guests in for dinner.

( )T ( )F   7. I would look forward to attending a party where
             I would not know most of the guests.

( )T ( )F   8. I would try a new solution to a problem at work
             that has never before been implemented in my
             company.

( )T ( )F   9. I occasionally make dates with friends before
             deciding ahead of time exactly what it is we will
             do.

( )T ( )F   10. I prefer to take a vacation in which we would
             drive around and stop at places that look fun
             and interesting, without a prearranged itinerary,
             versus traveling on a fixed schedule or tour.

( )T ( )F   11. I would try a new restaurant that looked interest-
             ing to me even if I knew nothing else about it.

( )T ( )F   12. I often try new or unfamiliar menu items when I
             go out to eat.

( )T ( )F   TOTAL RATING

Developed by Sharon L. Greenburg, Ph.D.; Used with permission.

Were you likely to engage in one area of risk far more readily
than another? Why do you think some areas of risk are more comfortable for you? Do you have a higher familiarity and competence
level in those areas? Does the risk level of your financial investments correlate with your risk tolerance in these areas? Why
might you be courageous in some areas of your life, but timid in
others, such as taking risks with your investments? What have you
discovered about yourself?

Perhaps you're more courageous than you'd realized. Perhaps you accept high risks with your investments, but are timid in your personal life. The risks we take and the successes and failures we make in one area of our lives will affect our ability to take on risk in other areas.

I do not like water sports. So what did I do? Signed up for private swimming lessons. Once I faced my apprehension over swimming, I felt, as the British say, rather chuffed, and headed to my office pumped up to make more sales calls and close bigger deals, even though none of that had anything to do with water.

What I have learned: Do one thing every day that scares you.

If you are uneasy about investing and feel the need to avoid risk like the bubonic plague, start small and build on it. Do enough research to find a conservative mutual fund in which to invest.[43] Once you get comfortable, research medium or high-risk funds or even individual stocks. You can train your risk appetite to get comfortable with different types of investments, and the reward will come. Pay attention to how you handle small failures. When you've learned to accept losses along with the gains, you'll be ready to take bigger steps.

You Are Called, and You Are Qualified

What makes up a successful money manager, and how can you be one? You needn't be an M.I.T. grad with a calculator for a brain and a penchant for reading financial reports on Saturday afternoons. Would it encourage you to know that wizards of Wall Street frequently overspend, undersave, and take ill-fitting risks with their money? There is no magic to investing and no guaranteed returns. Go past the hype, do not stop, do not collect $200, and advance directly to the facts.

Becoming a successful money manager requires little more than common sense, effort, commitment, and some savings to invest. Read a primer to learn about basics such as mutual funds, large and small company stocks, bonds, direct stock purchase plans, and dollar-cost averaging. The last item on that list is a simple but brilliant way to get involved in the market—simply making an investment of a fixed sum of money at regular intervals over time (such as once each month).

Every discipline has its foundational operating principles and it won't take long for you to get a good start. So, Miss Money Smart, aren't we glad Prime Minister Churchill rallied his beloved country long before they found themselves in a position of powerlessness? I'm proud that you're going to do the same. Pay attention while you spend, save, and invest. I learned long ago that a single dollar saved here and there, and then added to a few hundred dollars saved here and there, along with a bonus check here or a tax rebate there, adds up to real money, as they say. You can, and you will, build your own economic power, one dollar at a time.

CHAPTER NINE

The Trouble with Stuff

money and you

Take a moment to consider:

- Are your needs being met, or do you simply feel deprived?
- Do you believe God will meet all your material needs?
- Do you ask God to meet your needs? Do you ask God for what you want?
- Do you spend money recklessly? Do you spend with regard for a world of limited resources?
- If you had all the money you wanted, what is left that would be missing in your life?
- Would it trouble you if your neighbor, spouse, or minister saw exactly what you do with your money?
- How do you feel when you binge-spend or when you tighten up your cash in a frugal move; when your investments take a sharp dive or, conversely, when you see your savings grow exponentially?
- When you give money, what's the motivation? (Did the answer come quickly or was it difficult to know?)
- Is money your monster?

THE PROBLEM WITH MONEY IS THE STUFF IT BUYS.
Huh? Say that again? The thing about money is that you've got to
deal with the stuff you've bought with it. That is—you have to
spend your time and energy walking it, feeding it, vacuuming it,
polishing it, waxing it, lacquering it, downloading it, refurbishing
it, tuning it, and building a display case for it.

Then you have to spend more money to have it insured, repaired,
buffed, polished, detailed, dry-cleaned, repainted, updated, security-
alarmed, refinished, restrung. You have to buy the storage system to
organize it, the humidifier to protect it, the gear to outfit it, the display cabinet to showcase it, the custom bag to tote it, the software
program to manage it, the protective cover, accessories, leather case,
and then the remote to operate it from the next room.

Think about it: How do you expect to drive off in that new
Porsche without the appropriate shades and matching Porsche-
brand leather driving gloves? And then you'll need to join the
country club so you'll have some happening destination to roar
up to in that mean machine. Whew.

Ten years ago, I lusted over an expensive suit with exquisite

133

fabric and tailoring. It would have been a perfect upgrade for my wardrobe, which didn't include anything nearly so lovely. I told my colleague about the suit, and she said, "Better not, then you'll have to upgrade your entire wardrobe to that level of finery, otherwise you'll feel comparably frumpy on the days you're wearing your other stuff. Unless you're in a position to upgrade your entire wardrobe, you'd better stick with the clothes you have." She was right. Had I bought the suit, I'd have felt dowdy in the rest of my clothes and would be compelled to buy more designer clothes—which would have been stupid, given my income and long-term goals.

> You can't have everything.
> Where would you put it?
> ❋ *Steven Wright* ❋

This whole idea renders what a group of fishing guys in the New Testament did as almost appealing and certainly more understandable. Jesus said, "Come, follow me," and can you believe it if the career fishermen James, John, and Simon Peter didn't drop everything and do just that! "So they pulled their boats up on shore, left everything and followed him."[44]

Ouch! Just left their boats and gear, then and there, for the next beachcomber to discover. Can you envision a cause so compelling that you'd simply drop your capital assets and walk away? The idea is completely foreign to me.

As the frog that remains in water as it warms to a boil, so does the lure of lucre quite unnoticeably creep into our lives. Look over your to-do list. How does it compare with your chores of two, five, and ten years ago? How many of the tasks are simply taking care of stuff? Drop off, pick up, get repaired, buy batteries for, replace parts for, order new owner's manual to check instructions to recalibrate, reset, reclock, reprogram.

So *this* is financial freedom? Julia once explained poverty economics to me. Her family was struggling on a low fixed salary, yet inflation crept up, nipping at their well-worn heels. Said Julia, "We have much less to fear and to lose than the people we know with moderate, if not vast, wealth. We have so little downside, because we're already rather poor. We have discovered we can get by on the proverbial shoestring." Julia had honed an ability to appreciate small things and understood what Martin Luther King, Jr., meant when he said, "Only when it is dark enough can you see the stars."[45]

Julia recently said, "In a rather backward sort of way, we are at an advantage. If our wealthy acquaintances were to lose their jobs or hit an air pocket in the value of their investments, they'd have much farther to fall and greater pain to suffer. We, not they, live with lower risk and greater security. We already know how to get by on so very little."

> The deeper my crisis, the clearer my choices.[46]
> ⁕ *Andrew Boyd* ⁕

Stuff is like a pimp, robbing us of our innermost self, our soul, our serenity, and self-knowledge. I needed a fix today and bought two sweaters I didn't really need and a plastic briefcase just because it was cute and cheap. It feels good to get home and open the new packages. But my closets are full. If I lost everything in, say, a house fire, I'd have trouble remembering what it was that filled all those closets. If I couldn't remember what was there, how badly would I miss it, anyway?

Defining True Wealth

The values you established early in life affect what you desire and what you consider to be satisfaction of your needs. If your values include having great monetary wealth and luxuries, for any degree of peace and satisfaction, you're going to have to inherit, create, or steal—or else you must change your value model. It's going to be one or the other, or a default to the third option: a life of distress, dissatisfaction, and disenchantment. There are two ways to have enough. One is to get more; the other is to want less . . . or perhaps, want *differently*.

> Success is getting what you want. Happiness is wanting what you get.
>
> * *Warren Buffett* *

Adopting a less-is-more attitude has little to do with impoverishment. Rather, it is a healthy emotional state that comes from knowing what true wealth is and actively creating a life that reflects that definition. Living on less must be enjoyable and enriching, not a facade. Take the dieter who downs an entire chocolate cake after a week of celery and chicken broth. Such false asceticism will backfire, as in the case of the Spanish priest who took a vow of poverty but was later charged with smuggling $2.4 billion in counterfeit Treasury Notes.[47]

Create your definition of wealth. That is, what resources would you like in abundance? What is so sumptuous, meaningful, and significant that you would describe it as wealth? What does a rich life look like for you? In your life of wealth, where are you,

> E. Stanley Jones tells about a poor man who had an overnight guest, and as he showed him to his humble bedroom in the hay loft, he said: "If there is anything you want, let us know, and we'll come and show you how to get along without it."[48]
>
> * *Billy Graham* *

who are you, with whom are you, what are you doing, how are you being, how does it look, and how does it feel?

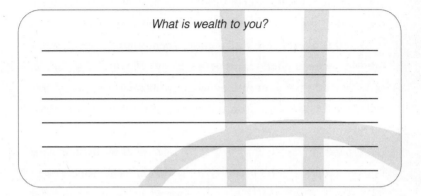

What is wealth to you?

_____

_____

_____

_____

_____

What Others Have to Say

Author Natalie Goldberg said, "I feel very rich when I have time to write and very poor when I get a regular paycheck and no time to work at my real work."[49]

Missionary surgeon Paul Brand said, "Because of where I practiced medicine [India], I never made much money at it. But I tell you that as I look back over a lifetime of surgery, the host of friends who once were patients brings me more joy than wealth could ever bring. . . . Now that I am old, it is their love and gratitude that illuminates the continuing pathway of my life."[50]

Author and Stanford Ph.D. David Korten wrote, "Money is not wealth. It is just a number in our head. . . . Real wealth is food, fertile land, buildings, or other things that sustain us."[51]

Emily Dickinson: "My friends are my estate."[52]

Mutual fund founder Sir John Templeton said wealth can be defined in one word: "Gratitude."[53]

Consider whether your day-to-day life expenditures of your

time, energy, and money are congruent with your definition of wealth. Is what you do, where you go, what you buy, and what you don't buy, a reflection of your life values? Would this be obvious to us, if we were all to hang out with you for a week?

Whether wealth for you is time, friendships, a sip of fresh-brewed coffee, a good tennis game, a day off, your baby's smile, or Bible study, put your money where your treasure is. Don't get sidetracked and spend it on the things you don't really value—things you don't truly want.

> Measure wealth not by the things you have, but by those things you have for which you would not take money.
>
> * Anonymous *

Beware this myopic view of wealth: Jack has never had enough. For years, he avoided his family's annual Fourth of July gathering because his brothers were medical doctors who owned luxury boats, cars, and toys. Jack worked in a ministry organization and didn't own much of anything. Although he loved his chosen vocation, he was embarrassed that his kids didn't have the stuff his nephews did. Every year he made the excuse to work through the holiday weekend so the other staff could have time off. Thus his family couldn't make the five-hour drive to his hometown. Traditionally, that was the only weekend his family got together; so for years, he, his wife, and kids missed all that rich family time.

I define wealth this way: It's a feeling, a sense of clarity. It's the ability to recognize your own value. It's the recognition of assets arranged in alignment with life values: freedom, friends, health, skills, personality; the ability to think, work, walk, breathe, and communicate. True wealth is a state of heart and a state of mind.

Are You Wealthy?

How do you know if you are wealthy? How do you know if you are blessed? Hint: Don't look for the answer on your bank statement.

Start keeping track. Do so in your calendar or journal. This is an especially valuable exercise if you're inclined toward a mite of self-pity or discouragement. Write down those things that "serendipitously" happen to you during tough times. Be aware and make note of the people in your path. Write down the word gifts they give you (lest you forget). It's so much easier to remember the bad words you receive and forget the good.

My latest gift was yesterday. Frustrated with my writing, I stopped in at Katarina's coffeehouse for some iced latte and inspiration. Of all the people in the city, who was sitting there nursing a coffee and a paperback? My old friend Mike Lipuma, whom I'd not seen in ages. For the next hour, I was incredibly blessed. Mike's an exceptional listener and thinker and loaded with just plain, straight-up smarts. Next morning, I noted that divine appointment in my calendar. Checking back through my calendar, I noticed exactly one month earlier I'd had a similar run-in with a friend from twenty years ago at a coffee shop in another state. Divinely scheduled appointments, I assert. The difference is, you enter them in your calendar after they occur, not before.

I've gotten in the habit of saving in my e-journal the rich blessings I receive via e-mail or in conversation. I was feeling particularly incompetent one morning until my friend Dave Jones cheered me by saying, "Sharon, you are *just* like Barbie—change your outfit, and you could do anything. Put on a pilot's uniform and I bet you could go fly a plane!"

When I started tracking these word gifts three months ago, I had no idea of the love I soak up every single day. I'm filthy *rich,* I've discovered! I'm filling them in as fast as I can write. My notes have begun to look like a financial statement documenting my wealth of friends and supporters. I've discovered blessings I get daily that I simply did not recognize and was not grateful for.

A Simple Life and a Rich Life: Mutually Exclusive?

Wherever you are on the money map—loaded with a bulging bank account, or hungry and just getting by—I propose you could spend much less money with no significant reduction in the quality of your life. *You* gain empowerment; *you* determine the strategies for frugal living with which you are comfortable.

Simplicity works. The best money manager incorporates the simplest of disciplines and methodologies. In fashion, a monochromatic look is most powerful and commanding. Such simplicity affords taste and a presence. This goes for interior design and the performing and visual arts too. Jil Sander and Armani fashions are long-lasting, despite the spin-cycle speed of fashion change—it's their profoundly simple lines.

Simplicity is empowering. Recall your college years, when you presumably had fewer possessions and fiscal responsibilities. Do you feel more entangled and trapped than in the era when there was less money and stuff cluttering your life?

Accumulating stuff for the emotional buzz does not correlate with long-term satisfaction. Air, water, parks, beaches, friendships, ideas, books, and health go a long way toward creating a sense of abundance, much of which is not about money and possessions. Likewise, a false sense of scarcity—when one cannot appreciate simple shelter, food, nature, or community—leads to unhappiness and distress.

People who have learned to live simply have often discovered wealth through other venues. They have countered material restraint with lives rich in culture and friendships. They understand the value of knowledge, the delight of literature, the satisfaction in gardening, the joy of intellectual conversation and repartee, the gratification that comes with volunteer work— particularly with people in greater economic need. There is so much human and cultural capital to be mined. Open your eyes to options for wealth far greater than financial capital.

> Don't let your possessions possess you.
> ☀ *Gloria Steinem's mother* ☀

Take me, for example. I decided to write this book without keeping a corporate job, draining me of the energy and creativity I need. I've adjusted with a simple and most gratifying lifestyle, but still schedule travel both domestic and abroad, a priority for me.

The thing is, having more brings more—more trouble, more anxiety, more responsibility. Even giving it away, if you've a lot, can be a source of great angst. The *New York Times* reported, "When John D. Rockefeller turned his attention to philanthropic causes earlier this century, he relied in many ways on his son, John D. Rockefeller, Jr., for help in deciding how to disburse his colossal oil fortune. Both father and son famously brooded, at times to the verge of mental exhaustion, over how hard it was to give away money in an intelligent and useful fashion."[54]

Are you aware of the golden handcuffs in your life? They're not just for C-level executives. They're everywhere. And they're constrictive. Money is a prison. Better to have less money, allowing you to break free to pursue the job you love, in a place you want to be, than fettered by golden handcuffs. They are hardly golden. In fact, it's possible they reek and you're quite unaware of the odor that permeates, left in your wake as you saucily stroll through a thing-filled life.

Generosity Keeps on Giving

May I let you in on a rarely understood truth—once again, a truth found in paradox. Giving is one of the least understood secrets to financial empowerment and satisfaction. It is a marker you cannot avoid along the road to financial freedom. The more freely you give, the less you will be constrained by the entangling roots of greed and avarice. The tighter your grip on your wallet, the more elusive financial peace will be. A spirit of generosity is essential for a full and balanced life.

> Those who don't [give] but could afford to are missing out on one of wealth's greatest luxuries.
>
> ∗ Andrew Tobias ∗

Can't afford to give? Don't believe the lie that you must earn more before you can give more, or that you must get out of debt before you can give. *Au contraire,* dear impoverished friend. Don't you know? It's the poor folk who are consistently more generous than the rich and often the wealthy who fail to give. One example comes from a politically prominent couple. In 1997, they reported a sorry $353 in charitable contributions on an adjusted gross income of $197,729.[55]

Anyway, are you not hip to the fact God gave you the ability to earn that little bit o' money in the first place? He could have allowed you to earn 10 or even 50 percent less than you do now.

Do you not know? Hope is all about magnanimity. So you feel poor? Give to charity. Do you struggle to get by? Contribute to missions for the needy. Do you feel defeated and depressed? Open your pocketbook and let the love flow out.

Financial writer Andrew Tobias wrote, "No one need give a penny if he or she doesn't want to. It's just that those who don't but

> The only way that money ever buys happiness is to give it away.
>
> * Jessie O'Neill *

could afford to are missing out on one of wealth's greatest luxuries."[56] I believe we all have a need to give because, as the Bible teaches, it frees and empowers our spirit and feeds our soul.[57] It's a good thing to give even when you don't feel like it. If you must, start with a speck and work your way up to more. The point is to start. You will begin to reap the benefits right away.

The Luxuries of Giving

The prophet Isaiah wrote that when you give, "Your light will break forth like the dawn, and your healing will quickly appear."[58] Get it? The recipients of your largess aren't even mentioned—the hungry, needy, and sick in Somalia, Appalachia, or across town. It's all about you and the healing and blessing you receive. In a reversal of JFK's challenge, may I suggest: Ask not what you can do through your giving; discover what giving will do for you!

Generosity is a means of grace. It lets us know who we are. Giving forces us to define our priorities. It promotes patience and discipline. Generosity wars against greed. Generosity deepens our faith. Giving teaches us to plan. In a world in which the majority of people have no choice about lifestyle, giving is an act of solidarity, allowing us to be consciously involved in the lives of others.[59] My neighbor Nathan says, "I just happen to like my view of the world. I know my spending involves a choice to spend on me or someone else. When I pay a dollar for ice cream, I'm simply aware of the fact that it's money I'm choosing not to spend on a hungry kid in Asia." No guilt about that ice cream; it's just that he and his wife, Shelley, have deliberately chosen a lifestyle allowing them to contribute 17.5 percent annually to charity. Because of that, they're conscious of what they do with the other 82.5 percent.

When we give, it brings us to the recognition that when we are squandering our money, we rob ourselves. Giving allows us to take a meaningful and significant stand against mindless materialism.

If you could use a little more light in your life to give you direction, satisfy your needs, strengthen your frame, and bring you peace, the prescription is clear: Give.

What You Believe Informs Your Behavior

Make a commitment to mining the truth about yourself, including the truth about yourself relative to money. You *do* know, don't you, that the value of your money has no bearing whatsoever on the value of you. When I *feel* incompetent, it helps me to think of the accomplishments I've had and kind deeds I've done. When I *think* I cannot do something, I check myself and correct those tainted thoughts.

How you think is everything. What you believe about money directly informs what you feel about money. What you feel about money directly informs your money behavior, and *that*, my friend, profoundly impacts your financial future.

There are *Facts* and then there is the *Truth*.

Fact	Truth
I don't have much money.	I have enough money for today.
I don't enjoy the luxuries my friends do.	I have what I need. I have not missed a meal this week.
I have no retirement savings.	I can open a retirement account today (unless it's Sunday—but Monday's coming).
My bills are overdue.	I live in a country where I am not immediately jailed or executed for nonpayment.
I experience anxiety, sleepless-ness, and relationship problems due to my overextended indebt-edness.	People like me—and worse—have overcome their debt prob-lems. I can too. I can call a credit counselor today.
I don't know where to start.	I can think of one little thing I can do differently with my money today.
I spend more than I earn.	I can change my perspective and desires and achieve true satisfaction.
I'm afraid I won't have enough money in my future.	I have the ability to make good choices with my money.
I feel incompetent and worthless.	I am a creation of God, lovingly and uniquely formed.

Commit to knowing your truth. Document the facts in your life, and think through the corresponding truths.

Fact	Truth

Let's face it: Stuff is exhausting—to buy, keep, and discard. We use things to get in the way of living our lives and don't notice when they begin to overgrow like a weedy vine that will soon entrap and immobilize us. In some sense, by having more stuff we reduce our freedom and choices in life. Try this test: Give some stuff away—lots of stuff, including money—and write how you felt about it. You'll be amazed. Jason gave his last hundred dollars to a friend who asked to borrow it. His sister exclaimed, "Why would you give away your last hundred bucks?" Jason said, "Because I didn't need it." Know what you need, know what you don't need, and discover the definition of true wealth.

CHAPTER TEN

Making Peace
with Money

money and you

Take a moment to consider:

- What do you want more than anything else in the world? What would it take to get that thing?
- What do you consider a financial crisis?
- Could money solve most of your problems?
- Do you have peace of mind?
- What void in your life are you trying to fill with money and things?
- Are you currently holding a grudge (having to do with money) against someone?
- How frequently in the last week or month has money caused feelings of anger, jealousy, or fear?
- When have you had to apologize on an issue about money?
- Can you think of any money you owe or that is owed to you right now? What feelings do you have around that?

YES, FRIENDS, THERE IS HOPE. IT IS TOTALLY POSSIBLE— in fact, it's probable that you can have a great relationship with all things money: the money you earn, the money you wish you earned, and the money you save. The money you spend, the money you drop in the canister at the checkout counter, the money you misplaced or lottoed along the way, and the money in your best friend's trust fund (yes, you've got to deal with other people's money if that's affecting you).

Money is just a thing—paper, really—but it's got the power of a nuclear weapon when we allow it to detonate our emotions, relationships, and decisions. When you've had lots of it, do you not feel quite so low when your boyfriend breaks up with you, when you gain another five pounds, or when your car breaks down? Does having what you perceive to be a lot of money make you feel powerful, in control of your destiny?

I definitely feel kind of fresh and strong and happy when I spend $89 at the outlet store to get four articles of fine clothing valued at $332. I feel better in new clothes. I even feel thinner in new clothes than old ones the same size. How about you?

Perspective

Making peace with your money is all about perspective. Yes! There is a better perspective to be had than the piteous one you have now (that idea of "If I just had a little more money, then my life . . ."). There is a perspective that can give you hope no matter what your problem with money. How do you get it? Move slightly. Simply reposition yourself so that you can see your situation from a different angle. What you need is to see exactly where you are, what you really have, and who you truly are.

Who you are is not about the money. What you really have is energy, brains, creativity, ideas, spirit, and probably some elements of family, home, love, friendships, a good reputation, work skills, talent, and the admiration of many. What you need is love that comes from relationship—relationship with the God who created you and has a plan designed for you, a purpose that makes a new plasma HDTV, trip to Cancún, and luxury car look piteously small.

You are bigger than stuff. You are bigger than getting caught up in the trinkets and clothes and possessions and furniture and knickknacks of life. Between the day you are born and the day they put your body down under, you ought to be something far bigger than a participant in the race to see who can get the most what. So meanwhile, what imprint are you leaving?

It's not about the money. It's about perspective.

Look Somewhere Else

When nothing in your circumstances changes; when your rent goes nowhere but up and your bank account nowhere but down; when you feel you'll be economically challenged for the whole of your life, that you'll never get rest from financial troubles—for the sake of life itself, *look somewhere else*. Why do you suppose some of the wealthiest people live in high anxiety? Like an anorexic teen of ninety-three pounds who sees herself as blobs of fat, they look in the mirror and see poverty and want. The bony teenager cannot see her gaunt flesh. She does not believe she is thin. The financial anorexic cannot see his prosperity. He does not believe he has wealth.

Such diseases of blindness are rampant. What irony, for we live in the richest culture in the history of the world! Most of us live in greater luxury than kings of great ancient empires. I believe the mental sensation (bordering on illness) of financial lack is perversely pervasive in our culture.

If it is a palatial home you lack, look in the mirror of health. If it is clothing and finery you're missing, look in the reflection of friendship and family. If it is food, shelter, and transportation that you need, look in the face of faith and spiritual sustenance. If it is a vacation home you want, look in the mirror of freedom of choice. If it is prestige you crave, look at the mirror of character to view your true beauty. Do you get it? Do you see the hope, freedom, and even fun that can be yours—this very day—for shifting your angle by even one degree?

Remember those makeup mirrors that ladies could order from the Sears catalog in the '70s? You could switch the lighting from day to evening and indoor to outdoor. The look of the makeup you applied varied greatly by which setting you selected. All you need to do is flip the switch to a different setting, and you'll see the ugliness or triviality of the things you crave and the beauty of what you already have.

Dear friend, the ninety-three-pound teen is not fat. If you've had a meal today and are expecting another tomorrow, you are not poor. It's often a long road to healing for the anorexic, but it can be a very short one for you. If you're mired in debt, like the anorexic who heals one bite at a time, your healing can happen, starting immediately, one dollar at a time. Monetary empowerment comes from the moment you adjust your view from lack to plenty, from poverty to prosperity, from want to wealth, from embittered to empowered.

Perspective tells us to look at what we do have, not what we don't. Looking over the fence is the mother of dissatisfaction, and the reason we shop. Perspective tells us that gratitude, rather than greed, is our appropriate response to money.

Unmasking the Myths

To make peace with money, you have to sort through the myths propagated about money. You have to get down to the truth. Before the first coin was minted, you see, myths about money (albeit in the form of chickens and goats) rooted around in the villages of early civilization, and have continued to perpetuate throughout history. Three of these assumptions continue to thrive like bacteria in a petri dish. We maintain a belief that money will reduce pain, eliminate our fears, and satisfy our desires.

Myth 1: Money Reduces Pain

The belief: If you had more money, you wouldn't feel the pain of loneliness, rejection, or uncoolness. The reasoning goes that you could afford the private Tae-Bo instructor and specially prepared foods to lose weight and become trim. Then you'd feel beautiful and attractive. You could afford fine clothes to hide your imperfections, thus looking gorgeous, attracting more friends, and having more love in your life. You could buy a successful company, thus gaining respect and power within the business community and government. You could afford a hot car and beautiful homes, which would attract a beautiful spouse who would be eternally devoted to you (a belief commonly held by guys, somewhat substantiated by the likes of Donald Trump's love life and Henry Kissinger's statement, "Power is the ultimate aphrodisiac"[60]).

But your pain, albeit briefly alleviated, will appear in other forms, because it cannot be annihilated by money. Indeed, money has been known to increase pain, elevate fear, and drive one to far deeper cravings.

I can hear what you're thinking: *Well, just a little more would make my life easier.* Perhaps, but if you believe that is true, I promise, you would need just a little more than that, and then a bit more, and the cycle would never end. To the question, "How much is enough?" the answer is perpetually, "More."

Internet entrepreneur Jim Clark's assets have numbered in the billions. When he was worth a mere $600 million, Clark had said, "I just want to have a billion dollars, after taxes. Then I'll be satisfied."[61] While building Netscape, his goal was to have $100 million, and before Silicon Graphics, what Clark really wanted was $10 million. Once his assets reached billions, was it enough? No. He wanted more money than the CEO of another company. When asked by a reporter if he wouldn't like to have as much as Bill Gates, Clark conceded that, for a moment, he would like to have more than anyone else."[62]

What drives Jim Clark? He seldom sees his mother and has never visited her in the home she bought with the stock options he gave her. His childhood was penurious and painful, and he determined to prove himself to his dusty little Texas hometown.

Enormous wealth has perhaps not satisfied his desire for affirmation or acceptance. He buzzes the little Texas town with his private jet when flying from his Palm Beach mansion en route to San Jose. Could it be that he pursues money, in part, to ease some long-ago pain? Do you suppose it is working?[63]

Myth 2: Money Eliminates Fear

The belief: If you had more money, you would worry less. You wouldn't fret about what others think of you and your career. You wouldn't be concerned about getting a promotion, a raise, fired, or a better-paying job. You wouldn't fear the future, wouldn't worry about losing friends, because people would flock to you if you had more money, because with more money, you'd just naturally have more style. (I actually saw this on television last night. A guy won $41 million in the lottery, and his looks changed overnight—from trashy to classy. His long greasy hair somehow looked movie-star suave when pulled into a long ponytail falling over his Armani jacket.) You wouldn't sweat it when the car breaks down, the medical bills arrive, or your mortgage payment and real-estate taxes drift higher. You'd never worry about interest rates.

> If I had known what it was like to have it all, I might have settled for less.
>
> * Lily Tomlin *

Or would you? I recently attended a posh soiree at which I met a lovely woman, dressed in a pale lavender gown that had a little swoop which trailed on the floor behind her strappy Manolo Blahniks. Warm and chatty, she described her career in Manhattan as a museum curator, which afforded her a home in Westchester County, trips around the world, and a nanny for her young daughter. The conversation turned to me, and I told her I write about money.

"Ohmigosh!" she exclaimed, her face shifting across an entire continent. The chic woman who was but a stranger seven minutes earlier softened her voice, lowered her head, and said, "I am terrified of money. I don't know what it is I should know about money, how much I have, or where my future is. I haven't even completed my tax filings for the year before last."

It was as if she had disrobed in the middle of the party. She continued, "I am a New Yorker. I know the subway system like the back of my hand, but every time I go to see my accountant, I get lost. My accountant's office, mind you, is just across from the Plaza Hotel. I know where it is. Everybody knows where that is. Yet every time I go to meet with him, I arrive an hour late. Again this year, I boarded the wrong subway train and when I got on the right one, missed my stop. When I rushed into his office, gasping for breath and apologizing yet again, he was quiet. When I settled down, he leaned across his desk and whispered, 'Miranda, I think it's psychological.'"

Talent, beauty, a fabulous career she loved, and money for a great lifestyle did not alleviate Miranda's insecurities. Another woman at the same party said she wouldn't feel really secure until she had ten million dollars. Only then would she breathe comfortably. As you might guess, her assets currently exceed a few million dollars, her income is strong, and her pocket is full of stock options that actually have value.

If you believe money offers security and freedom from risk of loss and can thus alleviate your fears, you need to know that banks fail. Fortune 500 companies collapse overnight. Pension funds dissolve. And, as in Miranda's case, lots of money brings its own fear-galvanizing problems. It can feel as secure as living in a mansion built square on the San Andreas Fault.

Myth 3: Money Satisfies Desire

The belief: If you had more money, you would be sated with power, vibrance, happiness, and love. You would buy extravagant gifts for your devoted friends. You'd feel great about supporting the Red Cross, homeless shelters, and disease research organizations. You'd get massages, facials, and manicures weekly. You would be fulfilled in your career and relationships due to the work with your psychotherapist, career coach, life strategy coach, and spiritual director, all of whom would meet with you regularly—to talk all about *you*.

All the pampering would make you feel complete. Diana-like, you'd be royalty. Foods would taste better, sights would be brighter, music more vibrant, and your relationships richer. Life would be a virtual heaven—a haven from sorrow, frustrated hopes, and unfulfilled longings. One would think Donald Trump might know. He said, "Whoever says money cannot buy happiness doesn't know where to shop."[64]

How is it you began to believe these lies? Probably in similar fashion to the way you got the idea that after marriage you'd live happily ever after. Such fairy tales were read to me before I could talk—years before my first heart-stopping, face-flushing crush in fourth grade on a boy named Ricky. Cultural forces, community values, and family dynamics all contribute to our beliefs. Even when we see evidence to the contrary—even when it comes as ice-cold reality like a whack upside the head, so are the beliefs we've held dear not readily abandoned. Did you not suspect there was no Santa Claus or Tooth Fairy long before you accepted that reality? You wanted to believe it, so you simply did.

Maggie was dying to get married. Although boyfriendless, her subscription to *Brides* revealed her aspirations. She moped until the day she got engaged, and then it was all about the perfect no-expense-spared wedding (although she felt the diamond was a bit small). Next she fixated on her desire to acquire. Maggie wasn't going to be satisfied until David bought her a mammoth house. Then she stormed until he upgraded her engagement ring. Then it was a second home, jewelry, world travel, and couture. Maggie felt an initial thrill with each new acquisition, but the half-life of the buzz got shorter and shorter.

The truth is that like an appetizer, money serves to wax your hunger for more. It's like salt, driving you to a crazy thirst. What will satisfy? What will make your dreams come true? It's not about the money.

> There are two ways to get enough: One is to accumulate more and more, the other is to desire less.
>
> ✳ G. K. Chesterton ✳

This is not news. We learn from King Solomon that wisdom is a more enduring satiation. In 1,000 B.C., he wrote, "With me [wisdom] are riches and honor, enduring wealth and prosperity. My fruit is better than fine gold; what I yield surpasses choice silver."[65] And "Better a meal of vegetables where there is love than a fattened calf with hatred."[66] Don't we know.

OK, so tell us again—*what is it you really want from your money?* What is it you think you can get with money? Complete the following sentences:

The most painful thing in my life right now is _____

_____.

I am most afraid of _____

_____.

More than anything, I want _____

_____.

In your private journal, list additional pain, fear, and desire you are currently experiencing. Write out your feelings about these issues and consider how your money behavior reflects those feelings. Write what you believe to be true about these issues. Write down some steps you can take toward a realistic resolution or healing of those issues.

What We (Really) Want

Let's dig beneath the surface of these emotions and desires.

The Good Thing about Pain

If all we experienced were love, happiness, and satiation, we'd not be of much use to the world around us or to ourselves. Pain keeps us informed. Pain offers valuable information, which is what keeps us alert, alive, and offers critical intelligence that we need to keep healthy, well, and to thrive. It tells us where things are wrong or out of order. It can keep us from dying, if we notice and attend to it. Proust wrote, "To kindness, to knowledge, we make promise only; pain we obey."[67]

The Good Thing about Fear

Fear keeps us alert to evil, mistakes, and wrongs. There is so much wealth to be discovered about accepting and managing fear and living with uncertainty.

> The beginning of anxiety is the end of faith, and the beginning of true faith is the end of anxiety.
>
> * George Müller *

The opposite of fear is faith. Faith allows us to face fear, embrace it, live through it, and not avoid it. Not to have fear is to be unmindful, naive, oblivious. Money can buy a security system, a bulletproof vest, and a private jet (reducing exposure to would-be terrorists), but money cannot buy bravery and courage. Money cannot buy faith.

The Good Thing about Unsatisfied Desire

We are actually nourished by desire as well as satisfaction. There is great value in desire. Desire tells us we are emotionally healthy—alive, innervated, and passionate. What would sexual satisfaction be without the predecessor of powerful desire? The arousal and anticipation—especially prolonged—is a significant part of the enjoyment, and essential to the ultimate satisfaction.

Let's face it: Pain is the empty, tortured feeling of being unloved. We want to replace pain with love. Fear is uncertainty, the expectation of discontent. We want to replace fear with faith. Desire is a deep yearning to be sated. It sprouts into greed, the need to stand out and feel special. We want to replace unfulfilled desire with contentment.

> The soul is nurtured by want as much as by plenty.[68]
>
> ✳ Thomas Moore ✳

How is it possible to achieve all that? Read on.

Admitting Our Powerlessness

You are not condemned to a life of want and, conversely, the struggle to overcome it. It is possible to see pain, fear, and desire transformed into love, faith, and contentment.

You can rewire your mentality to a new money reality. How is it possible to combat the urge for more and resist the G-forces of material desire that are fueled nearly every waking moment of our day? Fighting our feelings and motivations is neither easy nor healthy. Psychotherapists tell us to own our feelings. So rather than expend energy trying to suppress our urges, and rather than sabotaging our financial future by satisfying all of those urges, let's go for the third option. Reframe what you allow into your mind. Make sure what you think about and believe is true.

Reframing doesn't require huge willpower. Controlling feelings is difficult to do. But once you reframe your thinking, your feelings will follow. Controlling desire is nigh unto impossible, thus the first step in the Twelve Step recovery program: "We admitted we were powerless over alcohol—that our lives had become unmanageable." Have you ever reached a point where you've discovered the raw, bare truth about yourself—that you are powerless to control your desire for something?

I have been with and seen people in a place of powerlessness over an addiction in their lives. It is not a pretty place to be. Is money that something for you? Having faced and admitted my own powerlessness, having relinquished control over my desires to God, I was free to start my journey to recovery. Go to alcoholics-anonymous.org or debtorsanoymous.org to learn about the eleven additional steps to recovery. Are there areas in your life that are unmanageable for you? Is there an aspect of your money behavior over which you are powerless? Consider how the following statement would speak the truth about you:

I admit I am powerless over _____ —that my life has become unmanageable.

What we *can* do is discover the truth about God. We can seek fulfillment in relationship with him. Only God can affirm and love us through hardship, persecution, famine, nakedness, danger, and everything else in all creation.[69] Only God can satisfy desire. Only God can give hope. Only God can remove all fear. Only God can give true financial peace of mind. There have been times when my pain, fear, or desire have been so deep, all I could do was utter and meditate on those two words. Like a salve for my wounded heart, the knowledge that *only God* will make me whole, has lifted me out of tormented hours to hopeful days.

Look at What You Do Have, Not What You Don't

What we can control is our thoughts. So begin to look at and think about what you do have, not what you don't. Make a list and write it down. Start with the first item you use when you get up in the morning. The soft rug under your feet as you step out of bed. The heating and cooling system that keeps you comfortable, the book on your nightstand that is so enjoyable to read. The toothpaste that keeps you healthy and looking good, and the modern plumbing that makes it all so easy.

> My advice to you is not to inquire why or whither; but just enjoy the ice cream while it's on your plate.
>
> ✳ *Thornton Wilder* ✳

You might incorporate this in your journal. Each day, make note of a material possession that you are glad to have. Make note of a person or event for which you are grateful that day. Doing this each day will incite feelings of abundance, and starve your sense of scarcity until it slinks away, tail tucked between its sorry legs.

Reframing Exercise:
What Money Cannot Buy

What are the most exciting, memorable, and joyful things that have happened to you? Here are a few of my examples:

1. Age twelve, listening to the menfolk talk and laugh on Grandma's porch during a brilliant summer thunderstorm.

2. Getting my acceptance letter to business school. I shrieked and hugged a passerby in my lobby, mail sliding to the floor.

3. Hearing my first boyfriend tell me he loved me.

4. My niece Nora, who lives 2,000 miles away, bubbling over with excitement as she saw me walk toward her across the tarmac.

5. Sipping cold drinks while laughing and talking with a passel of friends on my back deck, late into a hot summer night.

> The habit of looking on the best side of every event is worth more than a thousand pounds a year.
>
> ✳ Samuel Johnson ✳

These thrills haven't much to do with money. I've not listed a new car, beautiful house, my first-class flight to Paris, or the Tiffany earrings from my sweetheart. (I ultimately misplaced both the boyfriend and the rubies. Truth is, he replaced me, but whatever.) Not job promotions and raises, or my biggest underwriting deal as a bond broker. These things were great, but they hardly compete with the list of most thrilling or satisfying stuff that's happened in my life. You know—those things that if I ever find myself in a POW camp, I'll want to relive in vivid detail to maintain mental and emotional acuity until the good guys come to get me out.

Quickly jot down your own list of the moments where and when you were most abundantly happy.

My Top-Ten Best Memories

1. _____

_____

2. _____

_____

3. _____

_____

4. _____

_____

5. _____

_____

6. _____

_____

7. _____

_____

8. _____

_____

9. _____

_____

10. _____

_____

How many of your most thrilling memories surrounded the
acquisition or pursuit of money and possessions? How many of
your best times had nothing to do with money? Did you list your
wedding day and the moment your child was born, or did you

mention the moment your insurance company agreed to pay for the baby's delivery bill?

Get yourself some perspective. Cut yourself some slack. Be gentle. If you make some wretched financial decisions, forgive yourself, and move forward. (You're not alone. Many a professional money manager has made the poorest of financial decisions.) If you can return that mink jacket or sweater you don't need, then do it, but if you've spent it on a cruise to Bermuda that caused you to miss your rent payment, don't flagellate yourself. Just move forward. Remember the admonition of my pregnant basketball coach: *Recover!*

> The things you really want, money cannot buy.
>
> ∗ *Rev. James T. Meeks* ∗

Inhale deeply, use your beautiful brain to analyze what it was that snatched your wallet, your head, and your heart in a moment of weakness, and be prepared next time to make a decision that will be better for the all-important, precious princess *you*. That dinner out, those titanium golf clubs, and that swell little orange TV for the kitchen counter are not worth shorting contributions to your retirement fund. The view from the larger perspective is a beautifully inspiring one.

> You may have a fresh start any moment you choose, for this thing that we call "failure" is not the falling down but the staying down.
>
> ∗ *Mary Pickford* ∗

Girl, make peace with your money. It beats war any day.

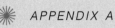 *APPENDIX A*

My Personal
Money Style

USE THIS QUIZ AS A COMPASS OF SORTS, TO HELP you pinpoint your location on the financial management map and figure out what you might choose to do differently. Remember, perfection is not our end goal. The objective is to raise conciousness—never guilt or discouragement. I'll be the first to admit that I cannot, nor do I ever intend to, check "T" on all ninety items on this list. My hope is that you will choose two or three of the items most important to you to work on this month . . . then another two or three to improve upon the next!

Check True or False

Maintaining

( )T ( )F   1. If available, I've arranged for automatic deposit of my paycheck.

( )T ( )F   2. I have a medical exam once a year and a dental exam twice a year. If gently aged, I have a mammogram and pap smear annually.

( ) T ( ) F   3. I have never postponed medical, eye, or dental checkups for financial reasons.

( ) T ( ) F   4. If I own my home, I have my furnace and air conditioning units checked each year.

( ) T ( ) F   5. In the last two years, I've had at least one pair of shoes resoled.

( ) T ( ) F   6. I have reviewed my long-distance, mobile phone, and ISP services in the last year to ensure the service is appropriate to my use (caller ID, call waiting, three-way calling).

( ) T ( ) F   7. I have the oil changed in my car at regular intervals.

( ) T ( ) F   8. I have set cash aside for emergencies, including several months' living expenses.

( ) T ( ) F   9. I have reviewed and, if necessary, updated my home and auto insurance in the last year.

( ) T ( ) F   10. I have reviewed my life, disability, and medical insurance policies in the last year; they are appropriate for my needs.

( ) T ( ) F   11. I know the deductibles on my insurance policies.

( ) T ( ) F   12. If I rent, I have a renter's policy on my stuff.

( ) T ( ) F   13. I have an umbrella liability insurance policy to protect my net worth.

Awareness

( ) T ( ) F   14. I know what tax bracket I'm in.

( ) T ( ) F   15. I have reviewed and understand my tax returns, or I prepare them myself.

( ) T ( ) F   16. I know what percentage of my income goes

toward housing expense. (I know the recommended percentages.)

( ) T ( ) F   17. I know what my net worth is.

( ) T ( ) F   18. I know how much debt I have.

( ) T ( ) F   19. I know my estimated Social Security retirement benefits.[70]

( ) T ( ) F   20. I've received and reviewed a copy of my personal credit report within the last two years.

( ) T ( ) F   21. I know how much my net assets have increased or decreased year over year.

( ) T ( ) F   22. I know how much money my spouse earns, how much my spouse is saving, and in what my spouse is investing as well as his/her debt load.

( ) T ( ) F   23. I understand the basic tenets of investing and know the difference between a stock and a bond.

Earning

( ) T ( ) F   24. I am fairly paid for the effort I put into my work.

( ) T ( ) F   25. My earnings keep pace with inflation.

( ) T ( ) F   26. I enjoy my work—it is well suited to my skills and interests.

( ) T ( ) F   27. I would not move to another job that brought me less satisfaction, even if it paid 10 to 20 percent more.

Spending

( ) T ( ) F   28. I shop with a list.

( ) T ( ) F 29. I make no more than two trips to the grocery store each week; I don't stop in, unplanned.

( ) T ( ) F 30. I buy items at twenty-four-hour convenience stores less than once a month.

( ) T ( ) F 31. I have a spending plan.

( ) T ( ) F 32. I buy used items from consignment stores or tag sales.

( ) T ( ) F 33. I use coupons at least occasionally.

( ) T ( ) F 34. I actually mail in the documents to receive rebate checks for my purchases.

( ) T ( ) F 35. I generally plan purchases in advance, buy bulk, and shop sales when appropriate.

( ) T ( ) F 36. I comparison-shop and research prices and quality before purchasing big-ticket items.

Borrowing

( ) T ( ) F 37. I keep a running total of the amount I've charged to my credit cards each month.

( ) T ( ) F 38. I use no more than two credit cards.

( ) T ( ) F 39. I use a debit card.

( ) T ( ) F 40. I know what the current interest rate is on each of my credit cards.

( ) T ( ) F 41. I pay my credit card balances in full each month—I have had no credit card interest due in the last year.

( ) T ( ) F 42. I have no debt other than my home mortgage.

( ) T ( ) F 43. I have never reached the credit limits on my credit card accounts.

( ) T ( ) F 44. I pay back borrowed money in a timely manner.

( ) T ( ) F 45. Because I plan ahead, I rarely get caught need-
ing to borrow money when out with a friend.

Paying

( ) T ( ) F 46. I believe I am responsible to pay my bills, even
if (errantly), I don't receive an invoice.

( ) T ( ) F 47. I have never paid my mortgage late, incurring
a late fee.

( ) T ( ) F 48. I regularly pay my bills by the due date or, at
minimum, eleven times out of twelve.

( ) T ( ) F 49. I have never been under threat of having my
car or other items repossessed.

( ) T ( ) F 50. I have never been under threat of having my
utilities disconnected for lack of payment.

Sensing

( ) T ( ) F 51. When I lose money (via investment, robbery, or
a hole in my pocket), I am stout-hearted, considering it a minor pothole in the journey of life.

( ) T ( ) F 52. When I lose a huge amount of money, I may
get upset or depressed, but within days or
weeks, I pick myself up, make adjustments for
the loss, and move forward.

( ) T ( ) F 53. When I see a friend with a new thing (car,
boots, coffee table, travel itinerary), I don't soon
find myself out shopping for a similar item.

( ) T ( ) F 54. I am unfazed by people around me who
seem to cash in on get-rich-quick schemes
via derivatives trading, IPOs, or MLMs.

( ) T ( ) F 55. I am in touch with my money reality—I don't worry about the future; I don't track my investments' performance daily or weekly.

( ) T ( ) F   56. I know my current cash flow—I know what's coming in and when and where it's going out.

( ) T ( ) F   57. I am aware whether the sum of money I typically withdraw from the ATM has inflated over time.

( ) T ( ) F   58. I am aware of the frequency of my trips to the ATM.

( ) T ( ) F   59. Because I plan ahead, I use only ATMs from my financial institution, thus incurring no additional fees for usage.

Saving

( ) T ( ) F   60. I know what percentage of income I save.

( ) T ( ) F   61. I set aside a specific amount for savings each pay period.

( ) T ( ) F   62. I save at least 10 percent of my income.

( ) T ( ) F   63. I contribute the highest possible amount to my retirement accounts such as a 401(k), 403(b), IRA, SEP-IRA, Roth IRA, or Keogh.

( ) T ( ) F   64. I take full advantage of my company's retirement and savings plans.

Recordkeeping

( ) T ( ) F   65. I keep my checkbook balance current.

( ) T ( ) F   66. I reconcile my checkbook with the bank statement every month.

( ) T ( ) F   67. I save and file my receipts.

( ) T ( ) F   68. I save and file my paycheck stubs.

( ) T ( ) F   69. I maintain a current file of all my tax information.

( ) T ( ) F   70. I maintain a current file of my retirement, pension, and profit-sharing information.

( ) T ( ) F   71. I track my medical bills and check them against the deductible owed and insurance payments.

( ) T ( ) F   72. I file my tax returns regularly; my tax payments are current.

( ) T ( ) F   73. I know where my records are: property records, mortgage records and payoff statements, automobile title, insurance policies, wills, trusts, tax returns, warranties, credit card info (account and phone numbers), and medical bills, etc.

( ) T ( ) F   74. I save ATM receipts and regularly record them within two days of the transactions.

( ) T ( ) F   75. Upon receiving a monthly credit card statement, I check the credit card receipts (which I have saved) for accuracy against the bill.

( ) T ( ) F   76. If I discover an error on my credit card statement, I follow through with the credit card company until it is corrected.

( ) T ( ) F   77. At any given point in time, I know my credit card balance within a fair amount of accuracy.

Giving

( ) T ( ) F   78. I have offered money to a stranger in the last year.

( ) T ( ) F   79. I tithe consistently.

( ) T ( ) F   80. I know what percentage of income I give annually to charity or church.

( ) T ( ) F   81. I am generous with my resources to needy causes or deserving folk who are down on their luck.

( ) T ( ) F   82. I have given money to a person who is home-less or in financial need in the last month.

( ) T ( ) F   83. When I give, I truly enjoy it, and I sense freedom as I share my wealth of resources.

Planning

( ) T ( ) F   84. I have a current will.

( ) T ( ) F   85. I have made and achieved specific financial goals in the past.

( ) T ( ) F   86. I have written financial goals for the present and future, including specific figures and dates.

( ) T ( ) F   87. I have a plan to achieve a financially secure retirement.

( ) T ( ) F   88. I have defined what a "financially secure retirement" means to me.

( ) T ( ) F   89. My spouse and I review our long-term financial goals and plans at least once a year.

( ) T ( ) F   90. I've done some thoughtful tax planning to ensure my investments, expenses, debt, etc., are appropriate to my tax situation.

My Personal Income and Spending Worksheet

Income Statement

Monthly Earnings—What Comes In

Salary and wages	_____
Dividends	_____
Interest	_____
Other investment income	_____
Child support	_____
Alimony	_____
Unemployment compensation	_____
Social Security, pension	_____
Other	_____

Expense Statement

Monthly Expenses—What Goes Out

Fixed Expenses

Rent / mortgage _____

Real-estate taxes _____

Condo association fees _____

Home equity loan _____

Auto loan _____

Auto expense:

    Gas _____

    Maintenance _____

    License _____

Insurance:

    Auto _____

    Health _____

    Disability _____

    Long-term _____

    Life _____

    Home _____

    Other: jewelry, boat, etc. _____

Education loans _____

Credit card debt payments _____

Other debt payments _____

Utilities (use monthly averages):

    Electric   _____

    Gas or oil   _____

    Water   _____

    Garbage removal   _____

Medications   _____

Alimony/Child support   _____

Child care   _____

House maintenance/repair/   _____

    alarm system

Savings   _____

Charitable giving   _____

Other   _____

Variable Expenses

Groceries   _____

Medical/Dental   _____

Tuition: education, other   _____

    skill-development, training

Professional services: legal, financial,   _____

    tax, personal counseling

Retirement fund   _____

Additional savings   _____

Other   _____

Optional Expenses

Phone: mobile/pager   _____

Cable, ISP, DSL   _____

Fees (credit card, banking)   _____

Pet care and supplies   _____

Sports equipment, fees   _____

Clothing   _____

Housekeeping/lawn care   _____

Dry cleaning, tailoring, repair   _____

Club and gym dues   _____

Leisure pursuits: dance, music, cooking,   _____
    tennis lessons, exercise class, etc.

Dining out   _____

Entertainment: films, theater,   _____
    sporting events, music

Books, periodicals   _____

Home furnishings and accessories   _____

Toiletries   _____

Barber/hair salon/spa   _____

Gifts   _____

Travel/vacation   _____

Other   _____

Recommended Reading

Randy Alcorn, *Money, Possessions, & Eternity* (Wheaton, IL: Tyndale House, 1989)

David Bach, *Smart Women Finish Rich: 7 Steps to Achieving Financial Security and Funding Your Dreams* (New York: Broadway Books, 1999)

Joe Dominguez and Vicki Robin, *Your Money or Your Life: Transforming Your Relationship with Money and Achieving Financial Independence* (New York: Penguin Books, 1999)

Jonathan Hoenig, *Greed is Good: The Capitalist Pig Guide to Investing* (New York: HarperCollins, 1999)

Ken Kurson, *The Green Magazine Guide to Personal Finance: A No B.S. Money Book for Your Twenties and Thirties* (New York: Doubleday, 1998)

Dr. John F. MacArthur, Jr., *Whose Money Is It, Anyway?* (Nashville: Word Publishing, 2000)

Rev. James T. Meeks, *How to Get Out of Debt and Into Praise* (Chicago: Moody Press, 2001)

Gary Moore, *Ten Golden Rules for Financial Success: Riches I've Gathered from Legendary Mutual Fund Manager Sir John M. Templeton* (Grand Rapids: Zondervan Publishing House, 1996)

Suze Orman, *The 9 Steps to Financial Freedom: Practical & Spiritual Steps So You Can Stop Worrying* (New York: Crown Publishers, Inc., 1997)

Thomas J. Stanley, William D. Danko, *The Millionaire Next Door: The Surprising Secrets of America's Wealthy* (Atlanta: Longstree Press, 1996)

Eric Tyson, *Personal Finance for Dummies* (John Wiley & Sons, 2000)

Web Sites for Financial Education and Information

bankrate.com—Bankrate.com, "Comprehensive. Objective. Free. Mortgage rates, CD rates, auto loans, credit cards, mortgages, and more."

bloomberg.com—Bloomberg.com, "Financial markets, commodities news."

crown.org—Crown Financial Ministries, "Teaching People God's Financial Principles."

debtorsanoymous.org—Debtors' Anonymous, "Recovery from compulsive debt."

fool.com—The Motley Fool, "Finance & Folly."

morningstar.com—Morningstar.com, "Independent help for successful investing."

myvesta.org—Myvesta, "The Financial Health Center. Get out of debt. Find happiness and wealth."

stockscape.com—Stockscape.com, "Investment Communities OnLine."

A Few Selected Web Services

amazon.com—"Earth's biggest selection."

cheaptickets.com—"The best kept secret in travel."

consumerreports.org—"Unbiased product ratings from the experts at Consumer Reports."

dealtime.com—"The shopping search engine. Compare products, prices, and stores."

ebay.com—"The world's online marketplace."

mysimon.com—"Compare prices and products from around the web."

priceline.com—"Name your own price . . ."

travelocity.com—"Go virtually anywhere!"

ubid.com—"Where you win at paying less."

NOTES

1. Ecclesiastes 5:10.
2. As quoted in Becky Tirabassi, *Let Prayer Change Your Life* (Nashville, TN: Thomas Nelson, 2000), 23.
3. Richard Ryan, interview by author, 26 August 2002.
4. Janet Lowe, *Ted Turner Speaks: Insight from the World's Greatest Maverick* (New York: John Wiley & Sons, 1999), inside cover.
5. Joyce Williams, "Where Are They Now?" *Decision*, May 2002, 30.
6. Scott Adams, interview by author, 3 September 2002.
7. Jacob Needleman, *Money and the Meaning of Life* (New York: Doubleday, 1991), 105.
8. Isaiah 55:2.
9. Pam Lambert, Michelle Tauber, and Alex Tresinwski, "After the Jackpot," *People*, 10 June 2002, 86.
10. *People Weekly*, 24 February 1997, cover.
11. Matthew Purdy, "The Money Doris Duke Meant for Charity Is Making Many Lawyers Rich," *New York Times*, 24 January 1997, Metropolitan Desk.
12. Judith Miller, "He Gave Away $600 Million, and No One Knew," *New York Times*, 23 January 1997, Metropolitan Desk.
13. See Ecclesiastes 5:19.
14. See Psalm 73:3.
15. Ann Lamott, "Dog Day," *Salon.com*, 24 June 1999.
16. Enid Nemy, "Metropolitan Diary," *NewYorkTimes.com*, 8 April 2002.
17. Matthew 6:24.
18. Humberto Cruz, "Savings," *Chicago Tribune*, 8 November 1996.
19. Ron Rapoport, *See How She Runs: Marion Jones and the Making of a Champion* (Chapel Hill, NC: Algonquin Book of Chapel Hill, 2000), 41.

20. Robert H. Frank, *Luxury Fever: Why Money Fails to Satisfy in an Era of Excess* (New York: The Free Press, 1999), 46–47.

21. Sarah Ivry, "The Cost of Being Alive: The Week-to-Weeker," *NewYorkTimes.com*, 15 October 2000.

22. Dan Benson, *The New Retirement: How to Secure Your Financial Freedom and Live Out Your Dreams* (Nashville, TN: Word Publishing, 2000), 43.

23. Bill McKibben, "The $100 Christmas," *Utne Reader*, November/December 1998, 62.

24. Jason Anthony and Karl Cluck, *Debt Free by 30* (New York: Plume, 2001), 50.

25. Katie Alvord, *Divorce Your Car: Ending the Love Affair with the Automobile* (Gabriola Island, BC: New Society Publishers, 2000), back cover.

26. Juliet B. Schor, *The Overspent American: Upscaling, Downshifting, and the New Consumer* (New York: Basic Books, 1998), 80.

27. James B. Twitchell, *Lead Us into Temptation: The Triumph of American Materialism* (New York: Columbia University Press, 1999), 101.

28. Paco Underhill, *Why We Buy: The Science of Shopping* (New York: Simon & Schuster, 1999), 168.

29. Enid Nemy, "Metropolitan Diary," *NewYorkTimes.com*, 11 March 2002.

30. Gary Richmond, *It's a Jungle out There: Humorous Tales through the Eyes of a Zookeeper* (Eugene, OR: Harvest House Publishers, 1996), 91.

31. As quoted in Laurence G. Boldt, *Zen and the Art of Making a Living: A Practical Guide to Creative Career Design* (New York: Penguin Group), xli.

32. Sophie Kinsella, *Confessions of a Shopaholic* (New York: Delta Trade Paperbacks, 2001), 27.

33. Ibid., 32.

34. Charity Crouse, "America, Land of Opportunity?" *StreetWise*, January 19–February 1, 1991, 1.

35. To have your name removed from mass advertisers' lists, write to Mail Preference Service, Dept. 5847793, Direct Marketing Association, P.O. Box 282, Carmel, NY 10512, or visit junkbusters.com. To reduce the number of incoming telemarketing calls, write to Telephone Preference Service Dept. 5847835, Direct Marketing Association, P.O. Box 282, Carmel, NY 10512. Include full name, address, and telephone numbers you wish to be deleted.

36. See John 12:3.

37. Lew Sarett and William Trufant Foster, *Basic Principles of Speech* (Boston: Houghton Mifflin Company, 1946), 417.

38. Proverbs 21:20.

39. Roger G. Ibbotson, Ph.D. and Peng Chen, Ph.D., "The Supply of Stock Market Returns," www.ibbotson.com, June 2001.

40. Peter Di Teresa, "How to Diagnose Your Portfolio," news.morningstar.com, 11 August 2000.

41. Jonathan Clements, "The Myth of the Dumb Investor," *Wall Street Journal,* 30 November 1998, R24.

42. Styrene is recognized by the Centers for Disease Control and Prevention as a neurotoxin and a possible carcinogen (see www.cdc.gov).

43. Well-established mutual fund companies such as Fidelity, Franklin, Janus, Scudder, or Vanguard are good places to start looking.

44. Luke 5:11.

45. Clayborne Carson and Kris Shepard, eds., *A Call to Conscience* (New York: Warner Books, 2001), 209.

46. Andrew Boyd, *Daily Afflictions: The Agony of Being Connected to Everything in the Universe* (New York: W. W. Norton & Company, 2002), 13.

47. Tom Hayes, "Priest Charged with Smuggling $2.4 Billion," *Chicago Tribune,* 23 June 1999, 136.

48. As quoted in *Billy Graham Answers Your Questions* (Minneapolis, Minn.: World Wide Publications, 1971), 104.

49. Natalie Goldberg, *Writing Down the Bones: Freeing the Writer Within* (Boston: Shambhala Publications, Inc., 1986), 48.

50. Philip Yancey, *Soul Survivor: How My Faith Survived the Church* (New York: Doubleday, 2001), 85.

51. Ellie Winninghoff, "100 People Who Have Changed the Way Americans Think about Money: David Korten," *Worth*, October 2001, 109.

52. A. S. Byatt, "A. S. Byatt's Bookshelf," *O*, March 2002.

53. Todd A. Sinelli, *True Riches* (Santa Cruz, CA: Lit Torch Publishing, 2001), 28.

54. Sam Howe Verhovek, "Elder Bill Gates Takes on the Role of Philanthropist," *NewYorkTimes.com*, 12 September 1999.

55. As seen on www.cnn.com/allpolitics/1998/04/15/gore.taxes.

56. Andrew Tobias, *My Vast Fortune: The Money Adventures of a Quixotic Capitalist* (San Diego, CA: Harcourt Brace, 1998), 165.

57. See Isaiah 58:10–11.

58. Isaiah 58:7–8.

59. Thomas G. Pettipice, *Visions of a World Hungry: Study, Prayer and Action* (Nashville: The Upper Room, 1979).

60. *New York Times*, 19 January 1971.

61. Michael Lewis, *The New New Thing: A Silicon Valley Story* (New York: W. W. Norton & Company, 2000), 260.

62. Ibid., 259.

63. Ibid., 262–266.

64. *U.S. News and World Report*, 9 January 1989.

65. Proverbs 8:18–19.

66. Proverbs 15:17.

67. Marcel Proust, "Cities of the Plain" from *Remembrance of the Past*, vol. 1, pt. 2, ch. 1 (New York: A & C Boni, 1930).

68. Thomas Moore, *Care of the Soul* (New York: HarperCollins, 1992), 191.

69. See Romans 8:35–39.

70. To request a Social Security statement estimating your future Social Security benefits, log on to https://s3abaca.ssa.gov/batch-pebes/bp-7004home.shtml or call 1-800-772-1213 to have a request form mailed to you.

SHARON DURLING IS A WRITER, SPEAKER, AND BUSINESS-woman living in Chicago. She was Vice President at a global financial services firm and graduated from the Kellogg Graduate School of Management, Northwestern University, with an MBA in Finance.

Sharon has a passion for empowering people with the truth about money—offering hope, direction, and inspiration toward gaining control of their financial present and future. Her desire is that others experience the freedom that comes with managing the uncertainty and letting go of fear about finances.

She speaks to women's groups, corporations, churches, and community clubs.

For contact information or to learn more about Sharon, please visit www.sharondurling.com.